A'ūdhu billāhi minash-shaitānir-rajīm.
I seek refuge in God from the accursed satan.

Bismillāhir-Rahmānir-Rahīm.
In the name of God, the Most Compassionate,
the Most Merciful.

Shaikh and Disciple

M. R. Bawa Muhaiyaddeen ☾

Shaikh
and
Disciple

Fellowship Press
Philadelphia, PA

This volume of *Shaikh and Disciple* is unabridged and comes to these pages directly from the words of M. R. Bawa Muhaiyaddeen ☮. Every effort has been made to keep the purity of his words intact. Nothing has been intentionally added, subtracted, or rearranged. It includes the discourses he designated for this book.

Library of Congress Control Number: 2018953559
Muhaiyaddeen, M. R. Bawa.
    Shaikh and disciple / M. R. Bawa Muhaiyaddeen ☮.
    Philadelphia, PA: Fellowship Press, 2019
    p. cm.
    Includes index.
    Trade paperback: 978-1-943388-43-1
    Hardcover: 978-1-943388-44-8
1. Allāh. 2. Sufism. 3. Islām. 4. Shaikh. 5. Guru. 6. Disciple. 7. 'Ilm.
8. Kalimah. 9. God. 10. Truth. 11. Good vs. evil. 12. Path to God.
13. Surrender. I. Title.

Copyright © 2019
by Bawa Muhaiyaddeen Fellowship
5820 Overbrook Avenue, Philadelphia, Pennsylvania 19131

All rights reserved. No portion of this book
may be reproduced in any manner without
written permission from the publisher.

Printed in the United States of America
by FELLOWSHIP PRESS
Bawa Muhaiyaddeen Fellowship
First Printing

Muhammad Raheem Bawa Muhaiyaddeen ☺

Contents

THE LESSONS	1
THE SHAIKH	9
THE DISCIPLE	29
THE LIGHT	39
THE LOVE	51
THE DIFFICULTIES	65
THE DANGERS	73
THE TREE OF TRUTH	79
THE JOB	91
THE FAITH	97
GLOSSARY	111
INDEX	119
M. R. BAWA MUHAIYADDEEN ☺	125

November 11, 1982
THE LESSONS

My love you, my grandchildren, my daughters, my sons, brothers, and sisters. May Allāhu, to whom all praise and glory belong, show us the way and grant us the grace so that our lives can become lives of absolute purity. *Āmīn*.

May He establish in our lives the proof of the truth known as the *dūlah*, the wealth, of His grace. May He establish the proof of the connection between Himself and us. May He establish the proof of the unity between Himself and us. May He reveal it to us and grant us His grace. May Allāh help us to attain this in our lives. *Āmīn*.

My children, we have now all gathered here together, have we not? For what reason? Love is the reason. The faith that knows how to find the way to peace in your *qalbs*, your innermost hearts, is the reason. Another reason—an intellectual reason, for instilling an awareness appropriate to the intellect—is for us to understand the nature of the connection between God and man in the time between our birth and *maut*, death, and to find a way to end the suffering in this birth. It is in this state that we have gathered here today.

We have been looking for a man of wisdom for a long time, for many days, many weeks, many months, many years. We searched and searched with the understanding that if we find such a genuine man of wisdom, we will be able to understand that connection.

Your intentions and faith have now brought us here. We have gathered together for that purpose.

When we gather in this way, that man of wisdom is a father to some of you—you feel the kind of love you feel for a father. For some, he is a brother. Some are grandchildren. Like this, the relationships exist in many, many ways: sisters, siblings, father, grandchildren. The little children call him grandfather. I have heard them saying this. The children before them called me father. This is what the children usually called me. Some call me *appā*.[1] Some call me guru. We use many words here like this. I have heard the children speaking.

Regardless of how many ways they speak of that relationship, we have all gathered together here for the purpose of love and unity. That is correct and good. Let us think about this state.

For a man of wisdom, there is only one point: the children, the daughters, the older children, and the younger children are *my children*. There is just that one statement. Where does that one statement originate? His heart. He has given birth to the children from his heart. He does not discriminate between children born from his heart. They equally share one part of his heart: the part of wisdom, the part of love, the part of his good qualities.

According to that state, all the children are in the same part. Because he gives birth to a child through compassion, he will have no bias towards that child or any other child. He will teach wisdom according to the innate nature of each child, according to his qualities, actions, conduct, and growth. He will give each child the food he requires. He will give each one the food and the protection he needs.

Children, you must not think of this as a *difference* or a bias. You must not think this. You must not think he is treating you differently. You do not have that measuring stick in your hands, do you? You cannot measure that section. Only the one who has measured the state of that child will know. Thus, you must think of this.

You must not doubt or measure to see if he gives you more or less food, thinking, "He gave me more. He gave me less. He spoke wisdom to me in a different way, and he spoke to another person in another way." You must not measure in this way.

---

1 *appā*   father, in the Tamil language

This is the thing that kills wisdom, love, faith, compassion, and unity. This is the thing that kills your purity. You must not develop it.

If there is a lack of wisdom, wisdom can come to dispel it; wisdom can dispel the ignorance. However, if you have what we just described, it is difficult to dispel. Why?

It is easy for the moon to dispel the darkness. It can drive out the darkness and shine. But if clouds join with the darkness, it is difficult for the moon to dispel them and shine. That section is like clouds in the darkness. If there is only darkness, it can instantly be dispelled and the light can shine. If clouds creep in and run across the moon, it will not shine with its full light.

Like that, if there is only a lack of wisdom, wisdom will dispel it. Yet even without a lack of wisdom, if those states exist there—if these clouds come to creep in—it will be very difficult for wisdom to dispel them. Those sections must not exist. You must throw them away. Although the sun may shine, if those clouds take over, it will be very difficult to dispel them. It is the same as it is for the moon—difficult for the sun to cut through the clouds until it fully rises. When there are no clouds, the light is immediately bright.

The wisdom you are studying is like this. If someone has a section of doubt, suspicion, and jealousy, it is difficult for wisdom, love, and faith to dispel them from his heart. Darkness can be dispelled, but it is difficult to dispel those thoughts. You must never have them on this path. If you want to walk on this path, you must not have those things.

The father of wisdom knows precisely what you need. He will watch you step by step and give to you according to your level of maturity. That father of wisdom will know. This is what you must reflect upon. Each child, please think of this. Those doubts must be thrown away. *My love you*, my grandchildren, my brothers, and sisters.

I will tell you something about my life. There are some lessons in the earth, some lessons in the ocean, some lessons in the jungle, some lessons in the ether, some lessons in the container that is the body of man. There are many lessons like this that we have to understand.

I myself had to learn a few of these lessons.

First, I had to learn what the ether was like. I studied the ether. Ether is defined as all the sections that can conceal us. Ether is the section that exists above our heads. Many clouds, many colors, many hues, many suns, many moons, many stars, many lightning bolts, many thunderclaps, rains, storms, and hurricanes exist within it, do they not?

Similarly, for our wisdom, the sections that exist above the mind are ether. These sections are the ether—this state is the ether. We see so many sections beyond the mind, do we not? Inside the mind there are four hundred trillion ten thousand cells, viruses, spirits, *shaktis*, or energies, maya, or illusion, darkness, and hypnotic delusions.

That which flies past our wisdom, beyond the control of wisdom, is ether. If you restrain these energies, they will be on the ground, on the earth. If you restrain the thoughts of your mind, they will be controlled and exist under you. When they are controlled, they become earth. Then they will be under your control and you can walk upon them. We can learn only if we take what is above us, place it underneath us, and walk upon it.

I went into the jungle. Many people were saying, "If we go to the jungle, we will be able to live with austerity and meditate in peace." Some spoke of going to the mountains, some spoke of going to the jungles, some spoke of going to the Himalaya mountains, some spoke of going to the ocean, some spoke of going to the caves in the earth—all places without people. They were saying, "If you live like that, you will be able to live with austerity and meditate in peace."

"Is that so? Let me go see that too," I said, as I went into the jungle. When I got to the jungle, there were countless snakes, beetles, worms, insects, wild fowl, and animals. There was more diversity in the jungle than there was diversity in the world. Elephants, lions, wild horses, wild pigs, jackals, and wild dogs were all there. They ran with me, ate their food, and slept. Some emerged at night and others emerged in the daylight to find their food. They caught and ate one another, killed one another, and ran in fear from one another. This is what it was like there.

"Very well," I said. "I too will go to join them." I lived in caves with them. I wandered as they wandered. I climbed the trees like the monkeys climbed the trees. When they drank from pools of water,

I watched them, and also drank. There was no difference. There was no difference between humans and the animals there. The animals did what humans did and humans did what the animals did.

"All right then," I said. There among the animals, I watched each thing that happened in every circumstance. I discovered the qualities and actions of each snake, each creature. I studied them. I did this for a long time. I studied the innate qualities and actions of each animal, its perception, its awareness, and its intelligence. I studied them to a certain extent. There was so much more—all the trees, the bushes, and the flowers. I came to understand each section little by little, little by little.

"Very well. This state is like this. It is not a place to meditate. This is not a suitable place for meditation and austerity. This is simply work that animals do. The animals live in a cave and the humans live in a cave. The animals go out to gather roots and fruit and so do the humans. There is no difference. The animals have not discovered what the humans are like and the humans have not discovered what they themselves are like. The human being in the jungle has not discovered what a human being is like and the animals there have not discovered it either.

"How can someone meditate if he has not discovered what a human being is like? It cannot happen."

I studied those things, went beyond that section, leaving the jungle, saying, "Let's take a little look at the ocean-creations." I entered the ocean, observing and studying them a little. The creatures there were also doing the same things.

"Very well," I said. I studied them, and then I studied the birds. They were the same. Some ate fruit, some ate worms, some ate insects, and some killed one another. One kind ate dead things while another attacked and ate what was not dead. They all had children, laid eggs, hatched chicks, and built nests, did they not? I observed them as well and studied their qualities. I studied their qualities and characteristics.

After that, I studied the animals in the cities. I studied them to discover the similarity between city animals and humans, and what sections would be there. I observed them. I observed the qualities of the city animals and the human animals. After I studied and observed them, I found that the city animals, the jungle animals, and the human animals were all the same. There was no difference whatsoever. They all did the same things.

The human being was doing everything the other created beings were doing. The human being had the same qualities and characteristics. He had what the monkey had. He had what the poisonous beings had and acted in a similar manner. He did not possess any section new to the animals and poisonous beings. Thus, there was nothing new here. Everything was the same.

It was in this way that I came to know the most difficult thing—to find a human being in the midst of all that was created. To understand the human being and to know him was difficult. "If after understanding the human being I were to understand God, it would be easy to worship Him and to meditate upon Him," I thought.

This can be done easily only after understanding. The lack of understanding was the difficulty. In the process of understanding, I had to understand the container that was my house and how to examine it. Thus, all those other endeavors were useless—none of them were meditation.

"Still, I need to find a place in which to meditate," I thought.

At that time I was told, "The house that was built for you and given to you is called the body." When I asked for a house, a place in which to do my meditation, I was told it was the body. "This body is only eight handspans in height. How can I live in it?" I asked.

"This does not apply only to you. Even an ant is eight-spans tall. Even an ant is eight of its own handspans in height. This is where the secret is. The body is an enormous school. It is your school, your house, your heaven, your hell, My kingdom, your freedom, your enslavement, your sadness, your happiness. It is a human being, an animal, man, and God. All the lessons exist within it like this.

"The body is an *en-sān* house, an eight-span house, and if you become an *insān*,[2] you will understand. If you become a human being, you can understand. That is the secret.

"You are the secret. I am the Mystery." That is what I was told.

In accordance with those words, I began to study the container.

"It will be good to know what must be discarded and what is

---

2 *insān*   human being

permissible for *insān* in this eight-span body. *Insān* has an eight-span house. You can become a human being if you understand the one-span house [the stomach] within the eight-span house, if you understand that place knowing that half of the one span is hell and the other half is the fire of hell.

"No matter where you turn after you understand these two halves, your earth will amount to just one handful—your heart.

"After you separate out what has gathered there in the heart, two spans will be gone—two spans will have been subtracted from the eight. After you understand and subtract those two spans, there will be six left. Of those two subtracted spans, half a span will consist of your sorrows, half a span will consist of your delusions, and one span will be the fire of your hell. Understand this.

"After you understand, you can understand the things you need in order to organize the remaining six spans in your house. What belongs to Me and what belongs to you? In those six spans, you can understand the secrets in all the eighteen thousand universes," He said.

"You can come to the sixth level of wisdom. You can become a human being with six levels of wisdom who can distinguish, differentiate, and understand, or you can become a worm in hell with one level of wisdom. You can become a *jinn*, a fairy, a demon, a ghost, or the five elements. You can become a *rūhānī*, a spirit, or even a ghost. You can become a human being, you can become My representative, or you can become My Light. You can intermingle with Me and abide with Me. The Two of Us can merge and live as One. You will know this to the extent that you understand it."

These were His words. As the understanding came, these were the explanations and words I came to know.

Thus, we must be *clear* about all that is hidden here and what it is like. This is what we must study.

It is certain that we must understand these lessons through a man of wisdom. He must be a man of wisdom and absolute purity, one who guides us with absolute purity in the search for our Father.

We, the children, will be able to know him only through that purity. To accomplish this, we must study wisdom with a pure *qalb*, with love, with unity, with faith, with harmony, and absolute purity. With strong faith, we can know the Father of absolutely pure wisdom. With that Father, we must study the purity with purity. That must be understood. That strength must be there.

With absolutely pure *qalbs,* we must endeavor to understand the secret of God who is our Father of absolute purity. We must endeavor to understand with absolutely pure love, with absolutely pure faith, with absolutely pure compassion, with absolutely pure unity, while leading a life of absolute purity. If we have that purity, it is certain that we will be able to understand that point and those lessons. It is certain that we will be able to understand that meditation, that worship, and those lessons.

If you—each child—can establish this state and understand, it will be easy for you to understand the connection between you and your Father. We will be able to easily understand, easily lead our lives, easily know what we need to know, possessing the wisdom and the actions to understand a life in which the Father and the children can live together.

That state itself is heaven. When the sections of love, wisdom, and unity merge, that is what is called the heaven of *gnānam*.[3] It is the heaven of *gnānam*, the heaven of *gnānam* in which the children that belong to the Father dwell.

When this heaven of *gnānam* is complete within us, it will be our Father's kingdom, the kingdom of absolute purity—*firdaus*. His beauty and Light and His kingdom will be given to us as a prize.

Thus, in the process of understanding, you must understand this state. You must understand this absolutely pure place. When you demonstrate the proof of this, it will be easy for you to reach your Father's kingdom, the kingdom of wisdom, the kingdom of love, the kingdom of compassion, the kingdom of patience, and the kingdom of *īmān*.

You must think about this. These are some explanations about the lessons I learned through my experiences. When the medicine for this works in a good section in your body, you will be able to see the goodness of it. If you consume bad medicine, it will torment you, and you will see only evil.

My love you. Please think of this. *Āmīn.* May Allāh help you.

---

3 *gnānam*   knowledge, knowledge of the divine

December 1, 1981
THE SHAIKH

My children, my daughters, my sons! On the journey of life, you must travel from the East to the West. It is a journey across a great sea, a journey upon a sea of maya, or illusion, a journey through jungles, a journey through deserts, a journey through desolate places.

As you travel on the journey of your life like this, there is a purpose. In that which is called life there are joys and sorrows, difficulties and losses, hell and heaven. Although you may go on many such journeys in your life, what you earn from them will depend on your own effort.

Regardless of the way in which those journeys may take place, in a God-life—in worshiping God—there is only one point: to obtain its sweet taste, you need to search with wisdom. And when you journey searching for wisdom and for liberation for your soul, you need a Shaikh who will find the wisdom and give it to you. He can point you to God on the map.

You have a Shaikh.

As you travel through life, you must move across so many things: joys and sorrows, the sea of maya, the sea of desire, the mind which is a desert in which nothing will grow, a jungle filled with animals— all of which is a dream. When you wake up, there is nothing.

You must get past the dream.

As you go, there may be many sorrows, blood ties, religious prejudices, and religious attachments. These are the jungles and seas you must traverse. It is difficult.

Yet when the difficulties arise, those who live in the ocean of maya will know nothing about those difficulties. They think they are comfortable there—the worms, insects, and viruses that live in the desert are comfortable there. Shade means nothing to them.

The monkey mind knows nothing about the difficulties in the jungle. It knows only that climbing up and down in the jungle makes it happy. The jungle is comfortable for the animals, as is killing and eating one another. The human animal does not know about the difficulties in the jungle either. Neither do the fish that dwell in the sea of maya. They are habituated to the difficulties.

However, a human being needs to know about the life of his soul and the freedom and happiness to be gained from it. If he wants to know, he has to walk.

If he comes upon a tree growing in that terrible heat, in the scorching sun, in the intense heat of the sun, when he proceeds on his journey like this through the jungle and into the desert where there is no shade—not a weed nor a blade of grass—the moment he sees the shade of that tree he will take shelter under it.

He will feel immensely comforted. He will be unable to allow even his foot to remain out of the shade. Under the tree there will be great comfort. There he will have great comfort, peace, and tranquility. He will be unable to leave even his foot out of the shade; he will fully understand the comfort and the discomfort of the shade and the sun. If he puts his foot out of the shade on one side, it will burn. If he puts his foot out of the shade on the other side, it will burn. If he stays in the shade for a little while, his fatigue and his exhaustion will disappear, and he will be very happy.

Will the insects, bacteria, viruses, and beetles that live under the tree and in its branches and leaves feel the comfort and the discomfort a human being feels in that same situation? They will not understand. It all seems like heat to them. They do not understand the comfort and the discomfort. Only someone who is searching and making that journey through the wild, someone who goes to sit there out of danger, understands its comfort. Only he will know—only he will know how rare and precious and comfortable that shade is.

This is what it is like for those searching for a Shaikh, those undertaking the search for God, those searching for truth and studying wisdom. If when they are making that journey in their lives, they find such a place—the shade of that tree, the Shaikh—they will experience immense peace as soon as they get away from the suffering and pain.

"*Ah*! How comfortable, how comfortable," they will say. Peace, tranquility, and serenity will come to them. If they are genuinely searching, that is how it will be when they get to that place. Peace of mind will come to them.

The search and the tenderness of the heart must be like that. If their awareness is like that, they will be comfortable. Then from there, they will be able to obtain a certain amount of peace and tranquility, alleviate their tiredness, and continue the journey of life.

After the sun and the heat have decreased, the Shaikh will remind you of the journey. "Now it is all right and you can proceed. Now it has cooled off and you can travel with ease. Look at the sky. Come, let's walk now. It is a cool time and now we can cross the desert. You must go through it and beyond it. Let's get past this mirage to what lies beyond. This is the suffering that comes to us. Let's get past it. Come," he will say as he guides you to another cool spot, and leaves. "Now you can travel easily, you will not be tired."

Those who do not search with tender hearts on this journey are like the beetles and bacteria and other things that dwell on the branches and leaves of the tree without knowing the comfort of the shade amid the difficulties of a journey. They will not understand the comfort and the discomfort. They are like beetles, insects, and bacteria.

Although they may be near the Shaikh, although they may dwell with the Shaikh like beetles and insects dwell on leaves, if they do not have this goal, this certitude, this section, they will be simply like these insects, unaware of the weight of life, that point, that kind of fatigue.

The effort of wisdom is needed: "I must reach the purity of the soul. I want God!"

Only if he makes a determined effort on the journey of life, only if he understands what happened earlier in his life and what will happen later, only if he understands the comfort and the discomfort, will someone know about the Shaikh—the shade of the tree. If he is unaware, he will not understand the comfort and the discomfort.

What is the use of being with the Shaikh if he is like that?

Such a person will be like a beetle on a leaf. He will not know how rare and precious the shade is. He will not know the precious value of the shade, how it comforts him and alleviates the fatigue of his journey.

Like this, no matter how many children may be with the Shaikh, if they do not possess that state, that certitude, that determination, that point, that understanding of comfort and discomfort, it will be worthless. They will just be like beetles. They will not go on the journey. They will fly in circles like beetles, and come back. Or they will be like parasites, sitting on the leaves and eating them. They will eat the world like that.

A genuine traveler will recognize how the shade that is the Shaikh will instantly comfort him. He will know the comfort. He will perceive the comfort and the peace. He will be able to obtain the comfort there in the daytime and continue from there to travel to the next cool place.

A Shaikh, a genuine Shaikh, will be like this. He will provide shade to comfort the travelers who are crossing the desert of the world.

Nothing will grow in the desert of your maya, your delusion. Everything in it is a mirage. If you see this mirage and think you are going to have water to drink, it will be just a dream. If there should be a tree in the place where you fall into that hypnotic delusion, it will provide the shade of wisdom. That is what a genuine Shaikh will do in the desert of life, where the dream of the mirage of drinking water exists. He will be there to comfort you, and to send you past that place. You will be able to know its comfort only if you possess that search, that certitude, and that state.

Then you will be able to know the shade of the Shaikh.

He will alleviate all the many difficulties that come to you. He will alleviate your suffering. He will alleviate your fatigue. If you act with awareness in this state, your journey will be easy. And your future journey will be easy.

Otherwise, you will be like beetles and insects. Even though you might be under the tree, you will make no effort. You will not understand the comfort. You will not understand the benefit. You will be comfortable just eating the leaves. If you live like that, you will not know the value of the Shaikh, you will not know the value of the wisdom. You will not understand the value of the comfort and you will regard it only as part of the sea of maya.

You must reflect, and after reflecting, you must understand the value of the Shaikh like this. You must think, "How much of my suffering has been alleviated by him! How much of the fatigue is gone! How much hardship is gone! How much comfort has come into the journey of my life! It will be easy to proceed from now on." If your certitude can be like this in a genuine search for God, you can obtain this comfort.

The Shaikh is the shade. This must be understood.

How should you be when you come to the Shaikh, when you are with the Shaikh? You must be very precise and subtle.

The Shaikh could use either of two statements:
- One is that wisdom can be like a bag of cotton. You can pile up many, many bags and bags and bags of cotton, yet they will not be heavy and they will have little value. You can fill many ships with it, yet they will have little value.
- The other is that a gemstone is a small *point*. The small *point* that is a diamond possesses far more value than a bag of cotton. A diamond is a great thing.

As for the cotton, there is a lot of it—it occupies a lot of space, yet it has little value. It takes up all the space so that everything else is hidden. It is not heavy and it has little value.

What does it take to destroy the cotton? A spark!

Similarly, no matter how much you accumulate in the world, it is all a dream, a bag of cotton. You magnify the dream world and turn it into a huge thing. You accumulate everything, everything, yet when you look at it, it is only cotton. If a spark touches it, it will be gone. The Shaikh has the fire of wisdom that burns everything. He can burn anything—anything you bring to him. He will burn it with wisdom. You must be careful in the presence of the fire of wisdom because cotton is a flammable substance. Wisdom can burn your life—all the ideas you have accumulated, your baggage, your thoughts, your religions, your ethnic groups, your blood ties, your relatives, your relationships, your associations, and your bondage to kinship. The wisdom of the Shaikh is a fire that can burn all these things. You bring with you a huge bundle, a huge bag of cotton. You have accumulated everything that belongs in the trash truck, and you carry it with you when you come to him.

He has a fire that can nullify all of it. He has something that can start a fire in your life. You are carrying four hundred trillion ten thousand bags of cotton. You come to him carrying so many shiploads of cotton. You spend all your time loading, unloading, and carrying them. You have bags and bags on the ship: how many days it will take to carry them, load them, and unload them, over and over again!

The Shaikh has no need to load and unload those bags. A small fire can take care of it, and it will be gone. He has less work. You have more work. He can burn everything with that fire, saying, "Now it is *clear*."

When you come to a Shaikh, he will have a fire that can burn all your baggage. He will have that wisdom. If you want to get rid of your baggage when you come to him, you must stay with him in an appropriate manner. You must sit in front of him.

If you are like beetles, what is the point?

The entire world is made of these accumulated bundles—life, the body, the world. You regard the world as a big thing, but it is a dream. Everything you see is a mirage. This world is maya's desert. You accumulated everything you saw in the desert, thinking that it would serve as drinking water for your journey. It is your dream—a mirage. You can never drink water from a mirage. The comfort will not come. The comfort will never come from it.

Your body is small.
The world is bigger than your body.
Your mind is bigger than the world.
Your desire is bigger than your mind.
Your karma is the biggest of all.
You have accumulated these things and that is your dream. You

have accumulated them and now you are dreaming. All of it is a dream. None of these things are of any use to you. When you go to a Shaikh, these things have to be burned.

Thus, you must sit there.

What the Shaikh has is very small. You have a truth within you and it is very small, but the Shaikh's wisdom is even smaller and extremely sharp. The truth is very small, but its value is great, and it is heavy. The other things are not heavy, they are just bags of cotton. The truth is extremely heavy. The wisdom of the Shaikh is very heavy and very valuable. The truth is like that. Truth? It is a very small thing. Wisdom is extremely heavy.

When you receive it, you must accept it with great care as he gives it to you. You must be very insightful. You must receive it knowing what it is and how valuable it is. Your strength must increase until it comes to a state in which it can carry the weight.

The strength that is faith, determination, and certitude must develop within you. Your hand must accept it with the strength of certitude, saying, "Oh! This is heavy, so heavy." When the Shaikh gives it to you, it will be heavy, and you must accept it with strength. Your *qalb*, your innermost heart, must accept it with strength. It is heavy.

If you accept it without strength, it will fall and break. It will be heavy and instantly fall to the ground. If you accept it without strength, it will be gone. If you accept it while you are carrying your bundles, it will be gone. If you accept it while you are carrying the dream of your mind, it will crush you, and what he gives you will break. It will fall to the ground.

What the Shaikh gives is very heavy. That point, that wisdom, is extremely heavy and extremely valuable. When you accept it, how must you receive it? You must commit all your strength to accepting it. You must have this strength and reach out with strength in order to receive it—*that* is strength. You must understand that the meaning the Shaikh gives you is heavy. You must understand its value. You must understand the weight of it. It is not a lightweight thing. You must understand the weight of it before you reach out for it. And then you must accept it with all your strength.

Your *qalb* must have this strength before you accept it. If you accept it like that, it will not be light, it will be heavy, heavy, heavy, the moment he places it into your hand. As soon as you place it into your *qalb*, it will be very heavy. Before you accept it you must observe that heaviness with a penetrating gaze. Only if you take that great weight into your *qalb* with this strength can you keep it where it should be kept. Then you can transport it to an appropriate place. Otherwise, it will break. It will break and you will fall.

It is then that the Shaikh will have to use one of two statements:

- If you accept it like this, carefully take it with you, and keep it in a safe place, you will be an intelligent person, a wise person, a mature person.

- If you playfully take what he gives you, it will break and you will fall. It will be gone and he will call you a fool. "You are a fool," he will say. "You do not comprehend this."

If you accept what he says, knowing its value, and if you keep it properly, he will say, "You are a wise person." He can use either of those two statements. He may tell you, "You are a wise person. You are a good child, a person of wisdom." However, if you put it down without knowing its value, he will say, "You are a fool. You have failed. You have missed the point. You do not understand its value. You are a fool."

There are just two statements. He will use one or the other: one statement for this and the other statement for that. You must understand. What the Shaikh gives you is very heavy. You must generate the strength—the faith, certitude, and determination—that can hold the heaviness. You must accept what he gives you with this strength. Then, if you do accept it in this way, you need to keep it properly. It is only with this strength that you can place it into *reserve*. That will be correct. If you do not act in that manner, you will be a fool who does not know the value of it. You must think about it. This is the way it is.

If you are with a Shaikh, you need to act according to why you came. You came searching for this. Very well. You must take it with a *point* that is commensurate with the heaviness.

Those who just come to sit with the Shaikh—and there are many of us sitting here, are there not?—will be like beetles sitting under the tree. Do they comprehend the comfort of the shade? They do not. They sit, they go, they fly away, they return. They will fly and wander about like Gnāniyār,[4] and return in the morning. They do not comprehend the shade or the comfort it gives. It is not like that. Only the traveler knows the situation—the difficulties and the losses.

Know the great value you receive from the Shaikh. The value will exist in each of his words; the value will exist in each point he makes; the value will exist in each of his actions; the value will exist in every gaze; the value will be there every time he takes your hand; the value will be there every time he places his hand on your head.

The value depends on the state in which he looks at you, touches you, and what he puts there. When he clasps your hand, there is great value in it. If he touches you in a certain way, there is a reason for it—there is something happening where he touches you. There may be a problem with your blood, a problem with your bodily fluids, a problem with your nerves, a problem with your hand, or a problem with your bones. That is why he touches you.

He will not touch you without a reason. You must think. There is a reason. The problem could be in your mind: in it, there could be lechery, hatred, miserliness, or thoughts of sex and the arts and sciences, so he will touch you with his hand. He will place his hand there in order to dispel those things. Then those things will decrease in you. There is an unseen benefit. Everything he does contains a benefit. He cuts things. He cuts those actions. He cuts those thoughts. That is another secret. There are certain reasons like this.

You must understand the benefit. If you stand in that place and observe the benefit, that will be the point. He will tap someone on the head. There is a point in it. In some circumstances, he will bang someone on the head. In some circumstances, he will hit someone on the head. In other circumstances, he will tap someone on their skin. There is a problem in each place. Only the Shaikh knows the secret. "Oh! It is this nerve, and it is causing this. It is the mind, it is causing this." Only he knows. That is why he may do these things. There are many reasons like this.

---

4 *gnāniyār*   A wise person. This is the name that Bawa Muhaiyaddeen ☮ called one of his beloved and long-term disciples, Nurul Karimah Mohamed, who left at night to go home to sleep, and then returned in the morning.

If his words are like this, and if you want to stay under him, your eyes and your intentions must be always focused on endeavoring to obtain the point.

There are times when the Shaikh is telling a *hadīth*, a tradition of the Prophet Muhammad ☮, and you go here and there in your mind even though you are here physically.

Some people go to the temple to look at clothes. They think, "Which sari is this woman wearing? Which sari is that woman wearing? Which sari is the woman over there wearing? Which blouse is she wearing? What kind of sari is it? What are her shoes like? What kind of jewelry is she wearing? What is her face like? What is her beauty like?"

They go to church to see those things. They go to the mosque and they look for those things, thinking, "What is she like?" Some people stand there and look for those things. Some look at the people while others look at the clothing.

Some look for relatives. "Who is here? Is my cousin or my uncle here?" Some look around, "Where is my child? Where is my little brother? Where is my child?" They look for those things. Others look around for what they can get, what they can steal. Some think, "What help can I get from that person? If I see him, what should I say to him, how can I talk to him?"

This is what we look for as we stand before God.

What did we go to see? We went to see God. We went to see God in the church, the mosque, the temple, or when we went to the Shaikh. This is the way some people are when they go to those places. They look around in order to see the world. "Is there a closet in the room? Is it like that? Is this here? Is that here? Is there a book here? What is happening?" This is what they look at. Even if a thousand years were to go by, this is all they would look at. "Who is coming in? Who is leaving?" This is all some people would look at even if a thousand years were to go by.

Someone who is like that does not look at what the Shaikh is saying. He is looking at other things. Some people are like that— some of them are looking at the ceiling, thinking, "What is up there?"

When the Shaikh speaks and makes his points, he looks at you.

The Shaikh is looking at you, but you are looking at other places. Your attention is upon other places. Your mind is focused on other places. When it is focused like that, you think, "There's a rat! A rat!" Those who are looking up are looking for rats in the rafters. "*Oohoohoohoo!*" you think, when you see a rat.

After the Shaikh has finished speaking, he will ask, "Is everything finished? Has everything gone in?"

What the Shaikh said did not go in because you were all looking at other places. Each person was looking at something else. The words did not go into any of you. There was no rapport. The words did not go into anyone. Nothing got into the people who were looking up. They just saw what they saw. They were looking up and smiling, but nothing went in. What the Shaikh said did not enter their hearts.

None of you said anything when the Shaikh asked, "Has everything gone in?" None of you were here. You had been thinking, "What does he have? What kind of sari is that? What kind of shirt is he wearing? What is happening in the world? What is that? How is the house? How is the yard?" That is where you were. You were looking up to see what was there.

One of the people who had been looking up replied to the Shaikh's question, "*Ah! Ah!* It went in, it all went in. Except for the tail! Everything else went in—just the tail is sticking out a bit."

The Shaikh asked him, "What is this about a tail sticking out?"

"I saw everything. I saw exactly how it came from over there."

"What came?"

"The rat! It came from over there. It stopped in that place for a little bit and then it started moving again. It circled around, then it stopped again and looked around, stopped again and looked around, glanced at all of us, and then crept into that crack. Look over there, only the tail is sticking out a little. The rest is inside."

"Oh! Is that what you were looking at? Didn't any of what I said get into you?"

"No."

"That's how it was?"

The rest of them didn't say anything.

"Weren't any of you here either?"

That person was looking at a rat creeping around in the rafters while the others were thinking, "What kind of saris, what kind of houses, what kind of properties, what kind of possessions, what kind of inheritances do the other people have? What is that person like? What does that person have? What does this person have? Is my cousin here? Is my mother here?" That is what they were looking at. Nothing the Shaikh said to them went in.

What benefit is to be gained from staying with the Shaikh in that state? Nothing gets in. What will saying, "I spent a thousand years sitting with him," accomplish? "I spent five hundred years sitting with him? I have been with him for fifty years." What is the benefit of that?

Does the rain fall constantly? No. We must finish sowing the seeds while the rain falls. We must plow what needs to be plowed, pull out what needs to be pulled out, and sow the seeds. We can obtain the benefit only at that time.

Is the Shaikh going to stay with you the entire time? No. You must grow the crop in that small amount of time. You must endeavor to grow the crop while the rain falls. Then you can benefit. The Shaikh will not speak with you the entire time. You must take the wisdom that falls now and grow your crops. Then you can obtain the wealth of the harvest that is your life. If you miss that time, you will not be able to grow your crops. You will be empty-handed losers.

You must pull the weeds and grow the crops while the rain that is the *rahmah*, the grace, falls. When the wisdom known as the *rahmah* falls, you must take it as it falls, accumulate it, and use it to grow crops for your soul. You must use the *rahmah*. Then you can reap the harvest. That is how you must search, sit, and reap the harvest in the presence of the Shaikh.

Otherwise, if one part of you keeps looking at the world; if another part of you keeps looking at ethnic groups, religions, and colors; if another part of you keeps looking at clothing; if another part of you keeps looking at relatives and relationships; if another part keeps looking for sexual experiences, possessions, houses, and property; if another part keeps saying, "I have learned;" if another part keeps saying, "I have recited, I have studied;" if another part takes pride in saying, "I have understood everything;" if another part of you keeps looking at blouses, clothing, jewelry, and other adornments; if you are in this state, nothing he says will go in. Your time will be wasted. This is not how to do it.

What he says must go in.

You must know the weight and the heaviness of each point. You must endeavor to accomplish this in your heart. You must always make use of each drop. Every point must fall into your heart and be used. The crop must be sown. Each *qalb* must be kept open and the points taken in. The water must fall there. The grace must fall there. The wisdom must fall there.

If only you could be like that.

Some of you are sleeping. Some of you are talking. Some of you are slouching and resting. Some of you are thinking of going back to America. Some of you are trying to go out *rounding*, thinking, "I should leave and do a little shopping." Some are thinking, "What is this? The Shaikh is just keeping us here in the house. He is not letting us go out. He is not allowing us to go out. I must grab a *broker* [a translator]. Maybe I can get Pillay to translate." Then you whisper to her, "Tell the Shaikh I want to go out for a little while." Others grab that man. Some grab Jean and quietly say to her, "Tell him I have to go out—to the bank, to the shop, to the post office." Some grab Gnāniyār, some grab Araby, some grab Mecci Tambi's wife[5] and ask them to translate. They grab them and whisper, "I want to go out. It is crowded here. I am tired. I want to go out and look around a little. I want to go out." That is what you are thinking.

It is all a waste of your time. Although you are here, these are your thoughts—your thoughts are about going out.

Even if a dog goes to the center of the ocean, it can only lick in order to drink. Even if a good Shaikh is pouring and pouring out honey to feed you, you are just licking it, "*Bla, lah, lah.*" If you have that dog inside you, no matter how much wisdom the Shaikh teaches you, no matter how much love he gives you, no matter how much compassion he shows you, you will only lick at it. You will go out and come back for a lick. No matter how much honey he gives you, no matter how much water he gives you from the ocean, this is

---

5 Pillay, Gnāniyār, Araby, Mecci Tambi's wife   These were some of Bawa Muhaiyaddeen's beloved followers in Colombo, Sri Lanka: Ameen Macan-Markar, Nurul Ameena Macan-Markar, and Nailahanam Macan-Markar.

what you will do—just lick.

If you have that dog and you do this, you will be thinking that you want to go out. Excrement is sugar to a dog. No matter how much you put in front of a dog, it prefers to search for excrement. That is what a dog will take in as it proceeds. Even if you use a chain, it will always pull you towards excrement. That is not the way. You will be gone. Only if you drive out this dog will you actually be able to be here. Only if you can be like this will the teachings go in. Then you can drink. Otherwise, you cannot.

Some of you have this dog.

Some of you sit here paying attention to other things. When you are with the Shaikh, you must endeavor to make sure that every drop falls into your heart. Some of you want to visit the world. You will not get this *rahmah* every day. You will only get a little for a certain amount of time. You must grow the crop during that time.

The meaning is not, "He will give it to me after I die." You must get the life while you are alive. It will only be alive while you are alive. It will only be wisdom if you get the wisdom—the wisdom contains the life. You must kindle the flame while you have the fire. If you wait until the fire goes out, you will only have lumps of charcoal. You must see the light while you have the motor and the machine. You cannot see the light after the machine breaks. Very little light will come from it.

Like that, what you comprehend when you are with the Shaikh, while you are still alive, is wisdom. What you comprehend after that is your mind—a dream. It will be like a dream. After that, you will conceive of wisdom according to what your mind thinks. You will think that whatever your mind tells you is wisdom.

When he is here, the Shaikh displays a fault as a fault, speaking to you directly, telling you, "This is wrong. That is right." If you can stay with him for every breath, every second—with this care—receiving every meaning, that will be your *hayāh*, your life, wisdom's *hayāh*, *gnānam*, the point. You must make this kind of effort. You must make this effort. Your eyes and intentions must have immense strength to receive what he gives. The crops will not grow within you while you go out *rounding*, circling here and circling there. They will not grow.

You must take in each point. Every point is heavy. Every word is heavy. Every glance is heavy. Every idea is heavy. They are heavy. You must take them carefully, put them into your heart, and grow the crop. Then you can obtain the benefit. You will not benefit otherwise. It will be too difficult.

Until you come to this state, you must correct yourself. You must have certitude in this state. Only then can you obtain the benefit. You must think of this. Nothing will get into you if you are like the insects and worms on the tree that live there without comprehending the shade. Nothing will get into you unless you pay attention to each word of the Shaikh and accept the heaviness. Half of you are going around the world while the other half are looking at the sky to see what is running up above. We must think of this.

After thinking, we must understand what kind of life we need to obtain when we are with the Shaikh. This wisdom is alive. This wisdom exists in a state in which it can understand and safeguard the life of the soul. You can obtain the benefit when you generate the state that is able to comprehend that purity. There are so many meanings in it.

Think about it. Why must you stay with the Shaikh for twelve years? Why do they tell you to stay with the Shaikh for twelve years? What is the meaning? You can learn to recite the Qur'ān in about two years. "*Oh, oh, oh, oh, oh, oh,*" you can recite it all. You can recite it with so many diverse melodies. You can learn to recite the Qur'ān in two years, yet you must stay with the Shaikh for twelve years. What is the meaning? What do you learn from the Shaikh?

You must study what he has. What kind of education is that? It consists of studying the qualities, the actions, the demeanor, the patience, the tolerance, the peacefulness, the tranquility, the serenity, the hunger, the wakefulness, the course of proper conduct, peace in the midst of joy and sorrow, the qualities in action, the compassion. Study the qualities. You must study his actions and demeanor. How he sits and his demeanor are the lessons. It will take twelve years to study the qualities, the actions, the demeanor, the *sabūr*, *shukūr*, *tawakkul*, and *al-hamdu lillāh*,[6] the peace, and the serenity. It will

---

6 *sabūr, shukūr, tawakkul,* and *al-hamdu lillāh*   patience, gratitude, trust in God, and giving all praise to God

take twelve years to learn this.

If you study these qualities, a fruit will begin to develop within you. The fruit of grace will develop in twelve years. You must generate his qualities and his wisdom. This is meditation, the twelve-year meditation. To study this for twelve years is meditation. This is the *purāna*.[7] To understand what is within yourself—your qualities—is the *purāna*. To recognize the wrong as the wrong, to push it aside, and to take in the good as the good—this training is the twelve years of study with the Shaikh.

That is how twelve years will go by. But that will not be enough to obtain *gnānam*.

Gnānam will appear only at the moment the cage known as *agnānam*, or lack of wisdom, is dispelled and the qualities known as *maygnānam*, or authentic wisdom, are established. It will appear only when the qualities of that which is known as maya are dispelled and the qualities known as God are generated.

The flower will bloom only when God's qualities take form. The moment the flower blooms, the fragrance will come into each petal. The fragrance will develop in each petal of that flower. As soon as those qualities reach maturity, the flower will emerge. When the flower emerges and the fragrance emanates, there is completion.

The moment the fragrance emerges, we will know what kind of flower it is—God's!

It will be God's son. God's daughter. It is the fragrance of God and that is how we know it to be a child of God. Then it is *clear*—it is His child. The flower is recognized by the fragrance. As soon as the fragrance is recognized, that will be the taste, that will be heaven, the kingdom of God. It takes twelve years to learn this. If you learn it, that is what will develop within the flower. The fragrance will come from it. The moment the fragrance emerges, the taste comes into it. It takes twelve years.

This is what you will be studying, nothing else.

To learn it, you must use wisdom. The entirety of the wisdom the Shaikh gives you is a knife. There is a jungle in your heart containing venomous creatures, cruel beasts, monkeys, vultures, animals that slaughter others, animals that catch and eat one another, animals

---

7 *purāna*   ancient history

that chase one another, animals that cause separation, animals that hunt one another, poisonous animals. The knife is for cutting away all of these things from within yourself, and for driving them out. You must drive them out and drive them out and drive them out, cutting and cutting and cutting away each one.

This wisdom is for driving out these things. This wisdom is for driving them out and nurturing the flower. Arrogance, karma, maya, *tārahan, singhan, sūran*,[8] lechery, hatred, miserliness, greed, fanaticism, envy, intoxicants, lust, theft, murder, falsehood, saying, "I, you, mine, yours," relatives, relationships, bondage to kinship, attachment, saying, "my religion, your religion, I am different, you are different," jealousy, covetousness, vengeance, deceit, treachery, speaking with one thing inside and another outside, not seeing that the hunger of others is like one's own, selfishness, hunger, illness, old age, and death, pride, envy, doubt, countless suspicions, anger, haste, impatience, sexual love, sexual attraction, the glitters, mind, desire, the monkey mind, hell, and all things like them must be cut away.

It is from the Shaikh that you must obtain the sword to cut away these and all similar things, to drive out all the demons and malevolent spirits.

You must wage a different war with each section. You must battle against them and drive them out. You must obtain the appropriate weapon, and drive them out. Each point of wisdom that the Shaikh gives you is a weapon of wisdom. You must use the appropriate weapon in each situation.

There is a specific weapon for the demons. There is a specific weapon for the fairies. There is a specific weapon for the *jinn*s. There is a different weapon for the elemental energies. There is a different weapon for the five elements. There is a different weapon for maya. There is a different weapon for hypnotic delusion. There is a different weapon for poison. There is a weapon that corresponds to each point like this.

As you pick up each weapon, you can operate on each disease. You can cut and heal it immediately. This is surgery you perform upon yourself. Only then will you be able to operate on your own

---

8 *tārahan, singhan, sūran*   the three sons of maya

illnesses. This is the wisdom that a Guru, a Shaikh who is an Insān Kāmil,[9] gives. It takes twelve years to dispel the evil, to assume God's qualities and the Shaikh's qualities, to put them into action, and to make them complete. That which will *clearly* tell you how to heal your illnesses in twelve years is wisdom.

That is wisdom—that is why you study *gnānam*. It becomes *gnānam* only when this is learned and the diseases are healed. Your *qalb* will have been made complete, the flower will have bloomed, and the fragrance will have developed. The fragrance itself is the *gnānam* that God will love.

That is wisdom and that is why you must stay with the Shaikh for twelve years—for the qualities. To learn the *vedas* and the *vedantas*, the scriptures and the doctrines, to learn the philosophies, to learn the *purānas*, to learn how to recite the Qur'ān, to learn how to read the Bible, can all be done in two years. Those things are easily learned.

It is difficult and rare to learn the good qualities. That is the meaning of having to stay with a Shaikh, an Insān Kāmil, for twelve years. This must be understood. If you do not obtain these tools while you have *hayāh*, if you do not obtain *hayāh* while he is with you, if you do not obtain his life with those tools during your life, or if you think, "We can obtain it after he goes," that will just be your mind's dream. It will be your mind's dream. You will dream and then afterward, you will say, "Oh! We forgot." It will be like that. You will not see it later. When you wake up, you will no longer see it.

However, whether you wake up and look, whether you sit and look, whether you walk and look, what you truly learn from the Shaikh will remain. That is not a dream. Learn it now. Now he can speak. He can speak of right and wrong. He can speak of good and evil. Now you can understand. You will not understand later.

If you genuinely study it now while you are here, you can speak of it in the future. Then you can speak of it when he is here and when he is not here. Now you must intermingle with him. Now you must intermingle with the words, the actions, and the wisdom. If you intermingle with them now, his words, actions, and wisdom will stay with you.

---

9 Insān Kāmil   a perfected human being

If you do not intermingle with them now, saying instead, "I will do it later," when will it ever happen? You will just have to keep dreaming. Your mind will have to keep dreaming.

You will understand only after you gather the wisdom and the qualities. Then they will be intermingled with you. This is what you must think about. Each child must consider this, reflect upon it, and endeavor to make use of it.

We will speak again later. *Āmīn*. Later.

April 23, 1982
The Disciple

My love you, my sisters, my daughters, brothers, sons, grandchildren, and granddaughters.

When a father or a Shaikh raises his children, he will contemplate the state each child will reach. From among ten million disciples, a Shaikh will look at the state of a particular child.

First, they will be people, then they will be disciples, and then they will become children. The Shaikh will observe everyone, all the people, all the human beings. After he observes the people, some of them will become his disciples. He will observe them carefully as they become disciples. After they become disciples, he will choose from them.

First, they are simply people. The Shaikh makes the selection from the people. After that, they become disciples. Only those whom the Shaikh selects become his disciples.

Then he makes a selection from among the disciples and they become his daughters and sons. He accepts them as his children. When he makes the selection from among the disciples, he observes the work they do in every section, and which section they accept.

We will give you an example of how he comes to select them. He analyzes them in this state and carefully observes the discussions in each heart along with their qualities, their actions, their nature, their conduct, the sounds they make, the way they sit, their behavior, their love, and their habits. As he observes the people and their conduct, he chooses for his disciple a child whose attentiveness, conduct, and state are *clear*. He selects from the people any child who is coming along correctly and makes him a disciple. Some of the people become disciples.

When making the selection from among the disciples, he looks at their qualities, wisdom, abilities, and awareness: "What kind of determination do they have? What strength do they have? What kind of effort are they making? What kind of awareness do they possess?" He looks into each aspect of the duty they do, the service they perform, and their prayers, observing in each aspect the state in which their determination is firm. Do they do these things hastily or peacefully? He observes them, selects them, and then makes those he selects his children.

After he makes them his children, he endeavors to make them *clear*.

How does this occur? When a woman gives birth, the child comes from the mother's belly. After she gives birth, she does not put the baby back into her body. It cannot be put back into the opening from which it emerged.

The Shaikh looks inside the child to see, "Is the point getting through to him? Is the understanding getting through to him? Is the faith getting through to him? Is the awareness getting through to him? Are the duty and the service getting through to him? Does he possess the connecting point between the current and the switch?"

Only if there is a connecting point can the lightbulb be installed and lit. This is what the Shaikh must analyze.

After he analyzes like that, he checks to see if the motor's current is passing through the wire correctly. "Can it be used and connected to certain places? Will it connect? Will it connect to the appropriate places or will the current be scattered by the motor?" That is what he will carefully watch for.

After he sees that the current is flowing and developing, he will check to see if the current can be used in at least one section. He will watch. "Is the connection developing correctly? Is this connection developing correctly in him? Does it connect like iron and a magnet?

Is he impatient? Is he angry? Is he hasty and foul-tempered? Is he jealous? Is he treacherous? Is he lazy? Or is he insightful and observant? Is he someone who possesses wisdom? Will the crop grow in the future? If it does grow, will it benefit many? Will it give peace to others? Or will it destroy others? Can the crop that grows destroy others? Will it be poisonous to others? When it grows, will it turn to poison or will it turn into tasty honey?" That is what the Shaikh will carefully observe.

If the Shaikh sees that the disciple's state is developing correctly, he will take him into himself, and make him his child. He will take him into himself and then examine him.

How will he examine him? He will prick each of that child's qualities. He will prick his every word, every quality, and every action and watch him. "Is this right? What state is developing within him?" He pricks the child to see what he will do, to see if he is suitable in each aspect. He pricks all those things.

If everything is appropriate, he will go even deeper to bring the child closer. He will examine him to see if he will turn out properly in the end.

How does he do this? Like a *vēdday vādi*, a hunter wasp.

This wasp flies alone. It comes into our houses to build its home. It builds its home of mud and then endeavors to hatch its young within it. However, it does not lay eggs. Instead, it goes out to investigate—to see if there is someone who will join its family.

"Which essence will become like me? Which point will come? Which kind of insect, which kind of caterpillar, which kind of beetle will become like me? Which one will join me? Which one will develop my qualities? Which one will develop my actions? Which one will develop my conduct? Which one will be appropriate? Will its wisdom, patience, and tolerance be appropriate? Which qualities will develop? Which one has the serenity to be able to act with those qualities? Which one will take my form?" This is how a hunter wasp will proceed.

There are tiny, tiny greenish-white inchworms that live on leaves and drop down from a thread. The thread is in their mouths and they drop down like spiders and crawl on leaves. They have their own forms, they eat leaves, and they drop down from margosa trees.

The inchworm is beautiful. The wasp pricks each inchworm like that, and watches. It pricks each one of the inchworms and insects. It pricks them a little with its stinger.

If the inchworm wiggles too quickly, the wasp says, "This one is not good. It is an impatient one," and leaves it. The wasp looks around further and pricks another. That one may run away from him very fast. The wasp thinks, "It is hasty, very hasty. It does not have the ability to take in every word and merge with me. It will run away and leave me. It will run from certain points. It will not stay in my house. It will not obey. If a small point comes, it will not be able to bear it and it will run away." So the wasp will leave it.

It will prick many other caterpillars and insects. One of them may not say or do anything, even after one or two pricks. After the wasp pricks and pricks it, the wasp will say, "This one is not very special. It lacks ambition and awareness. No matter how much I say to it, it will not join me. It is a bit dull-witted. This one is not right for this."

The wasp will prick a few more insects and caterpillars. Some will lie there doing nothing, even though the wasp pricks, and pricks, and pricks them. "This one's awareness is absent. It is witless. It has no wisdom or intelligence at all. It is completely insensitive. Nothing will enter those ears. This one is the worst of all," the wasp will say after it pricks it.

The wasp will go on to many others. One of the inchworms it pricks may move away from the place in which it was pricked. It will move gently. It will move and check the place in which it was pricked. It will move in a very gentle way, moving away from each place in which it is pricked. It will move gently.

The wasp will say, "Do you want to go on a journey?"

That inchworm will say, "Yes."

"This is the right one," the wasp will say, accepting it immediately. The wasp will then take it to the home it has built. It will put it inside and close the opening with mud. The wasp will bring mud, close the opening, and fly in a circle. Every day, it will fly in a circle, saying, "Become like me! Become like me! Become like me! Become like me! Become like me!" Its words are, "Become like me! Become like me!" The wasp watches like this for forty to ninety days.

It flies around and when it returns, it checks to see if the inchworm has turned into a wasp. The moment it becomes a wasp, it gently bites and bites and bites through the mud, breaking its way out of the nest. As soon as the wasp hears the sound, it comes to enlarge the opening. Then the new wasp emerges. By then its form will have become that of a wasp. It will have the same form and the same shape as the hunter wasp. And then it will begin to do the same work the hunter wasp did. It will do the work that it did.

Like this, when the Shaikh is choosing a disciple, he makes the selection first from among the people. Then he chooses from among those he has made disciples as he pricks and pricks and watches them. He pricks each one. As he pricks them one by one by one by one by one, he watches to see which one to choose, which one will become *clear*.

He observes every aspect of each one of them. "This one is an angry man. That one is an impatient man. The one over there is dull-witted and there is no use telling him anything. This one is a talker. That one is someone with no awareness. This one will obey what is said but it will not penetrate; his ears do not hear. The one over here will linger wherever he goes. That one is an impatient man, constantly touring the countryside. This one will sit but he will not study; he will sit but he will not understand."

The Shaikh will carefully watch them all. He will prick them like the hunter wasp. He will prick each one of them until he can say, "He is all right. He will correct himself. He will come out all right."

He will make that one his son, his child. That one will become his son or daughter. When the Shaikh makes someone his daughter or his child, he raises that child in the same way the people in the world give birth and raise children. As he raises them, he pricks and pricks and examines each one.

He is the mother.

He will raise the children with his wisdom, good qualities, actions, conduct, and nature in this section just as a mother raises her children. If he has ten children, he will raise those ten children in that way and in that state. "Which one will develop that ability? Which one will do the work that I do? What will he do? What duty will he do? In what way will he act? Will he be patient?" That is what he will look for.

If the Shaikh has chosen him and if he comes to this state, that child will be his child and the Shaikh will raise him in his own nest. Just as the hunter wasp chooses an inchworm-child, puts it into the mud nest, and closes up the opening, the Shaikh takes the inchworm that is the soul, the truth of a child, and places it into his own nest, into the house of his heart. He places the child into his heart and teaches him.

"Become like me! Become like me! Become like me! Become like me!" he says. He places the child there, and teaches him.

For twelve years, he teaches him God's words, God's actions, God's conduct, God's patience, God's love, God's compassion, unity, peace, tolerance, and how other lives are like his own life. He reveals all the sections that are there. He places that child into his own body and shows him each component.

"Within you exist countless qualities, countless animals, countless demons, countless ghosts, *malā'ikah*, angels, germs, viruses, cells, blood, gases, liquids, and fire." The Shaikh will put him there and give him the explanation of each one. He will give him the explanation inside and outside.

He will keep his son and daughter outside and teach them. He will also teach them inside his body. He will place them into the absolutely pure heart of his soul—into his soul—and teach them inside and outside. He will show them and present these things to them externally and also internally. Externally, he will show them the example of the structure, internally he will show them the substructure.

The Shaikh will teach the child's soul, his wisdom, and his heart from the inside. "Stay here," the Shaikh will say. "Stay here and learn. All the things you see in the world are things that are here inside you. Look here, all the points of the world are within you. Look here, all the darkness of the world is within you. Look here, all the fire in the world is within you. The animals, birds, fowl, demons, ghosts, *shaitāns*, snakes, scorpions, beetles, wasps, the sun, the moon, the stars, and all things are within you. Four hundred trillion ten thousand *spiritual* deities, the mantras belonging to the demons and ghosts, and all the astrologies are here. They are contained within these five letters. Look at them.

"There is no enemy in anything you see outside. All the things you see within yourself are your enemies. They only seem to be outside. The outside is simple. We cannot see our actual enemies outside—those are just common, ordinary objects [to which we ascribe attributes]. All your enemies are within you. All the enmity is there. Do you understand?

"These are the enemies you must conquer. Look here inside yourself. Sit down. What is that sound? It is a snake. What is this sound? It is an elephant. Look carefully. It is an elephant in rut. Those are the forces within you. What is this sound? It is a tiger. Look at it jump with a leap of your mind, as it seizes things. What is this sound? It is a horse, running a race. What is this sound? It is a bull, plowing up the world, wandering about, and carrying burdens.

"What is this sound? It is an eagle. Look at it flying high above—look, in the clouds. It is watching to see what lives below, to see if there are any snakes or rats. What is this sound? It is a vulture searching for dead bodies to eat. Dead bodies!

"What is this sound? It is a goat. What is this sound? It is the sound of deer and elk. That is a moose. What is this sound? It is a mountain goat. What is this sound? It is a python that captures things. What is this sound? It is a dog that howls at night. What is this sound? It is a stork. What is this sound? It is a crow. It caws loudly, saying, 'This is unity,' repeatedly making the same sound. All one hundred five million created beings, countless created beings, are making the sounds. What is this sound? It is a monkey. They all make sounds.

"Where are they? All those sounds are within you. All those sounds are in man. Each animal possesses its own particular sound, but man is the world—man himself is an immense world. All the sounds are within him. Did you hear the sounds? Those animals must be transformed.

"Man is the worst animal. He is the one that kills all the rest. He is the one that makes all the sounds. He makes the sounds, calls to them, and kills them. He caws like a crow, and the moment a crow comes to him, he kills it. He bleats like a deer, and as soon as a deer comes to him, he kills it because of his selfishness. He trumpets like an elephant, and as soon as an elephant comes to him, he kills it. He neighs like a horse, and as soon as a horse comes to him, he catches it. He seizes everything for his own use. He possesses all the sounds.

"No other creation lives like this.

"For his own selfishness, for his own food, his own stomach and hunger, man does the work of controlling all things, all created beings, with these sounds. Those sounds must all be transformed. He must destroy the sounds with which he calls to them in order to kill them, and begin to peacefully regulate and control them instead.

"Then he will have no enemies. After cutting away the enmity, he must give those forces work. He must give each being work and provide it with duties to do. He has to bring them to the habit of doing duty.

"You should neither become a slave to them nor should you destroy their lives. You must regulate each thing. Fire can be extinguished with water. Water can be blown away by air. Fire can control many things. Air can be controlled by a mountain. Water can be controlled by mountains, hollows in the ground, rocks, and hills. It is like this that you can control each thing with another.

"You must control the five elements. Earth, fire, water, air, and ether can all be controlled by each other. When you control all five, you will discover that the entire world, all the creations, all the sounds exist among these five. You must discover this."

The Shaikh will say this and show you examples. After he places you into himself and begins to raise you, he will show you everything. As soon as the child learns there in the correct way, he will have no external enemy or opposition at all. After the correct wisdom is taught to each aspect of all the beings there inside him and they learn to do *khidmah*, service, and duty, the outer things will be simple. They will all do duty to him. There will be no enemies.

This is the state in which the Shaikh will teach the children. He will show them and teach them, keep them inside himself, and raise them.

Outside, he raises their bodies. Inside, he raises their souls.

He will place wisdom, the good qualities, and actions into them, and raise them. This is how he will raise them. He will endeavor to make them like himself, just as the wasp does with its children.

He will place a person of wisdom there and raise him.

The Shaikh will raise him there, and as soon as he becomes his child, those qualities will become God. As soon as those actions, qualities, and wisdom come to God's section, he will give that child to God, saying, "You raise him now."

After the child learns all the Shaikh's qualities here, he will be taught God's qualities there, and from then on, he will be [merged with] God. After he learns all the qualities, he becomes God's child.

Then God will teach you from within Himself. The Shaikh will place you within God, and then he will be within you, teaching you, finally saying "Now you are right."

That is the state in which he will teach you.

The Shaikh will give that child to God. He will make his own child into God's child, and then give him to God.

This is the way in which the Shaikh will select each point until the child can finally come to that state. After the Shaikh has transformed the child to be like himself—to possess those qualities, those actions, and that form—he takes him and transforms him into God's qualities and actions, and then gives him to God, to grow within Him, saying, "Raise him. Protect this treasure and raise it."

This is the Shaikh's section: pricking and watching and watching and watching and watching, making and making and making and making the choice in each place as he takes the child to God's section.

There are not many children. There are only a few.

He does this one by one by one by one. A Shaikh will prick you and watch over you like a hunter wasp. He will prick and watch each child, each one. He will prick and watch each quality. He will prick and watch each action.

If when he pricks, the child leaps up and makes a fuss, the Shaikh will leave him. He will leave him, saying, "*Ah!* That one has these qualities. This one has those qualities. That one has those qualities. Danger will come from him. Danger will come from him as well. Danger will come from him too. He will harm the others. He will kill the others. He will cause enmity among the others. He will sin against other lives." So the Shaikh will reject those children.

These are the teachings of a Shaikh, teachings of his experience. If he is a genuine Shaikh, he will keep you like that. That is how he will choose you.

There are many explanations like this. How much there is to examine! A genuine and wise Shaikh will examine so many people. He will prick and prick and watch them with wisdom. He will do this with wisdom, with love, with good qualities and actions. He will prick them and watch them and make his choice. This will occur in each section. May we think about this.

If you think about it and stay there in the right way, you can be raised properly. Then it will be right.

You must understand this, children. If you grow in this way, learn, gain clarity, struggle, make the effort, and develop the care, the awareness, and the actions, he will select you. He will choose you and teach you.

At one time, he may keep you outside, telling you, "Observe and look at this." At another, he may keep you inside himself. When he keeps you inside, he will teach wisdom. Outside he will teach you about your mind and your body.

You must think of this. *My love you*, my daughters and sons. Think of this. Do you understand?

August 3, 1981
THE LIGHT

THE SHAIKH
We must control the horse so it goes where we want it to go. Do you understand? Hold the reins correctly. If you have caught the horse, hold the reins properly. If you want to catch the truth, catch the mind. To search for truth, catch the mind.

A DISCIPLE
That's easy to say, but every time I'm going, I feel like I'm going on the right path, it seems like I always get bowled over by grief or sadness. It seems like I was going okay, and then everything explodes.

THE SHAIKH
There is a leak somewhere. When there is a leak, the water will not accumulate in the pond. The leak has to be fixed if the pond breaks when a small thing happens.

THE DISCIPLE
The leak is not something that can be controlled from the outside by fasting or any outer action. It can only be controlled from the inside.

THE SHAIKH

The water is inside, not outside. The water is in the pond. The leak is in the wall of the pond. That is the difficulty and that is why it breaks. If there is a leak in your faith—a leak in your *īmān*, your faith in God—it will break your mind and your life.

THE DISCIPLE

That's what I came here for. That's the reason I came to Ceylon.

THE SHAIKH

That is what must be controlled.

THE DISCIPLE *(laughing)*

Do you have a pill or something I could swallow?

THE SHAIKH

I am giving you that pill every day. I am giving you a pill every time. You must swallow these pills correctly—these [discourses] are the pills.

If a mustache grows on your face, you need a barber to shave off the hair. If the hair grows inside you, you need wisdom to shave it off. If you want to shave off external hair, you need a barber to shave you, to make you look nice.

You need a barber and his sharp blade. The knife is very sharp, so you must sit properly. Then the barber can easily cut off the hair. If we sit properly, he can do his work in an orderly way. If we move, we will be cut. It is not because of his cutting. He is careful.

However, the knife has no such consideration. It simply cuts. Therefore, the one who sits must sit properly. The barber will do it correctly. He will endeavor to hold the knife carefully. He cannot be blamed if we make a mistake in sitting. The knife is doing its natural work. Its sharpness is doing its natural work. Its work is simply to cut, so it cuts. It is not the barber's fault. It is not the knife's fault. The knife is sharp. The way we sit is at fault. We must think of this. We are not sitting properly.

Similarly, wisdom is very sharp. The shaving must be done very carefully. We must sit in a state of faith and certitude. We must sit in the world with real faith and certitude. The point that is truth must be there—truth without doubt. The hand of truth must hold the wisdom, and the hair that grows in the mind must be shaved off. It must be shaved off inside. It must be made beautiful. Just as the face and this and that are made beautiful externally, the inside must also be made beautiful. Make faith, certitude, and determination strong. Then the shaving can begin.

Without them, no matter how much truth there may be, if you look here and there as the shaving takes place, if your certitude moves here and there, the knife will cut you and there will be an accident. There is no fault in the truth; it is natural for the knife to cut. If you fail to be still, it will cut you. If the angle is wrong, it will cut you. The angle must be correct. Then you can be made beautiful. If the one who sits does so correctly, the barber can shave correctly.

The Shaikh will give you that beauty. He will hold the sharp blade and make you beautiful. He will do it, but the knife is sharp and you must sit properly. You must have that strength. Then he will make you beautiful. He will make your *qalb*, your innermost heart, beautiful with that extreme sharpness. The knife will cut you if there is a failure in the certitude of the one who is sitting. That is the pain. That is the reason the pain comes to each of you—you lack certitude. The blade is sharp. *My love you.* Be strong. That is the leak in life.

What else? *Love you.* What else would you like?

Fire will not last in water. Like that, when you are on your way to God's section, when you are going there in order to bathe to obtain a sense of well-being, do not take the fire of sin known as the world with you. Do not take this mind with you, thinking to make it *clear*. Taking the fire with you will not make you feel well. The fire will be extinguished and you will feel hurt. What is this? It cannot survive there—it is fire. You must use your wisdom.

THE DISCIPLE
Oh! Last night I had a dream about a fire burning down a house.

THE SHAIKH
That is what burned the house. Do not keep fire inside the cage [of the body]. Do not put fire into that cage. It will burn down the house and that will not be good. When you are in the process of

becoming *clear*, do not take fire with you. Do not seek help from fire. Whether it is the world or karma, it is fire: hunger-fire, sin-fire, karma-fire, desire-fire. *My love you*, child. You must think of this. All those things are fire.

The world is the fire that makes man suffer. The world is the fire that destroys him. All his thoughts are fires. His intentions, thoughts, desires, attachments, possessions, inheritances, bondage to blood ties, religious bigotries, languages, colors, complexions, love, hunger, old age, illness, death, selfishness, doubt, anger, haste, impatience, and jealousy are all fires.

THE DISCIPLE

I'm going to recognize jealousy, because I just *(laughing)*—

THE SHAIKH

Ah! There are fires of jealousy, saying one thing on the outside while keeping another inside, ignorance, speaking without knowledge, desire for land, woman, and gold, and countless others like them. We kindle countless fires like those. Countless fires. Man lies burning in those fires every day. He does not spend a day without that heat. The child, the calf, the cow, and the house are fires. Possessions, comforts, all those things are fires. He burns in those fires every day. Arrogance, karma, maya, *tārahan*, *singhan*, *sūran*, the three sons of maya, lechery, hatred, miserliness, sexual infatuation, fanaticism, envy, intoxicants, lust, theft, murder, and falsehood are all fires.

These fires of sin burn man every second. He lives entirely in fire. Man lives in fire, worse off than an animal. He is continuously burning in fire, continuously ablaze. This is hell. He lies writhing in this hell, shouting, smiling, weeping. If it cools down a little, he says, "*Ah!* It is nice and cool now," yet he will cry the next second, "*Oohuhuhu!* I can't bear this." This is what he has discovered in his life.

There is a saying: "A good Guru Nādan, a True Guru, does not kill, he does not kill. When a good Guru Nādan hurts us, he does not kill, he does not kill." He is there to dispel our horrible qualities. He is there to kill each of the qualities that feed the fire. That is what the Guru does. By doing this, his work is to make you peaceful.

Yet as he cuts off each horrible quality, one after the other, we say, "*Aiyō*! I'm attached to this. *Aiyō*! This is my love. *Aiyō*! This is my mother. *Aiyō*! This is my grandfather. This is my father." There is pain, much pain as he cuts off each one. "*Aiyō*! This is my friend, my boyfriend. This is my teacher at school, my school, my nice house." As he cuts each of them, one by one, there is pain, pain. As he *clears* out each place, you may feel anger, rage, hatred, confusion, doubt, and suspicion.

When a good Guru Nādan cuts each one of those things, this is what may occur. This is not done as a killing, it is not done to kill you. He is treating you to dispel your horrible qualities. This is the reason.

"You are burning in the fire, are you not? Yet you think it is good for you. But it is a fire and it is burning you. You think it is good, but it is a tiger drinking your blood. You do not understand. That is your ignorance. Observe it with wisdom," he will say.

That Guru Nādan will cut away each of the four hundred trillion ten thousand *spiritual* demons, *spiritual* fires, *jinn*s, *malā'ikah*, angels, fairies, deities, demons, ghosts, elemental forces, four-legged beasts, monkeys, asses, rats, peacocks, crows, pigs, dogs, jackals, lizards, crocodiles, chameleons, and armadillos.

Armadillos have the strong grip of a monkey, and it will hurt if they grab you. The more you beat and beat and beat an armadillo, the more tightly it will hold on. When you beat the mind with wisdom, it will hold on even more tightly. When you give it advice, it will hold on even more tightly and hurt you even more. That is what an armadillo will do. It possesses the monkey-grip of arrogance, and it will hurt you even if you use wisdom to try to make it let go.

When an armadillo grabs the trunk of an elephant, the elephant will not be able to breathe very well, nor will it be able to bear the pain. It will trumpet. It will trumpet very loudly. An unintelligent elephant will beat and beat it against a tree, but the armadillo will only hold on more tightly. The elephant will run and keep beating its trunk against the trees, but it will seem as if a spiked chain were attached to it. The armadillo will only hold on more tightly and the elephant will not be able to bear it. The armadillo is extremely strong. An unintelligent elephant will beat it against trees and rocks.

The more the armadillo is beaten, the more its strength increases.

A wise and intelligent elephant will also run and run the moment an armadillo grabs it. A wise elephant will think, "There is nothing I can do to it, but there is a way for me to escape from it." A wise elephant will run and run and run to a pond and put its trunk into the water. It will hold the armadillo under water, the armadillo will not be able to breathe, and then it will let go, leaping and scrambling up to the surface, thinking, "I have to get away!" The intelligent elephant will run to the water, thinking, "I must escape."

Similarly, once we know what is holding on to us, once we identify it, we must use wisdom and immerse it in God. We must immerse it in faith. We must immerse it in truth. Intelligence and wisdom will immerse an evil action in true things. Then the evil action will let go all by itself and run and run in order to escape.

Ignorance, however, will try to beat it against the earth, the rocks, the maya, the fire, this quality, and that quality. It will beat it against everything—against its bondages, relationships, desires, attachments, and blood ties—but the evil action will only hold on more tightly. It will beat and beat it against religions, ethnic groups, and colors, but its grip will simply increase.

That is not how it can be done.

The evil action must be immersed in truth, wisdom, and *sabūr*, patience, and then it will let go of the elephant and run away on its own. That is the point. That is how it is done when an armadillo grabs hold of you. It is a monkey-grip of stubbornness and arrogance. "*Hah-hah-hah-hah-hah!*" the monkey will say as it charges at us. Can we ever win that battle? We must do it without a confrontation. Then it will say, "*Heh-heh-heh-heh-heh!*" and run away.

Wisdom will act in that manner.

A Gnāna Guru, a genuine *Truth-Man*, a good Guru Nādan will do this. Because of this, you will feel pain as each section is being cut away. You will immediately feel pain as he cuts away each section. The pain will come to that mind. The pain will come to that desire. The pain will come to that attachment. The pain will come to that intellect. The pain will come to those thoughts. That pain will come, but he must cut—that is what a good Guru Nādan will do.

It will hurt, but you must think, "A good Guru Nādan will hurt me, but he will not kill me, he will not kill me. He is doing this to dispel my horrible qualities. This is a fire I myself have set. He is doing this to put out the fire." If you examine what he does in detail, you will see him cutting away the fire that has been burning and consuming you.

He will be cutting away the fire known as your karma. He will be cutting away the fire known as your hunger. He will be cutting away the fire known as your doubt. He will be cutting away the fire known as your arrogance. He will be cutting away the karma of the five elements of your birth. He will be cutting away all the delusions you hold within you that are mesmerizing you. He will be cutting away the fire known as desire. He will be cutting away the monkey mind, the seventy battalions of monkeys—seventy battalions of monkeys! He will be cutting away your connection to these monkeys. He will be cutting away your connection to this body. He will be cutting away the connection to lust. He will be cutting away the connection to your anger. He will be cutting away the connection to envy. He will be cutting away the connection to jealousy. He will be cutting away the connection to impatience. He will be cutting away the connection to everything you reach for without careful consideration. He will be cutting away the division between the "I" and the "you."

You will feel the pain as he cuts each one, each one, each one. The pain will come to your mind. There will be no pain for wisdom and truth. The opinions you hold in your mind will feel the pain. Your thoughts will feel the pain. Your desire will feel the pain. Your blood ties and attachments will feel the pain. As he cuts and cuts and cuts, all these things will feel the pain.

The pain is the reason you find fault with an Insān Kāmil, a *Truth-Man*.

He is not in business. This is not a business for him. His work is cutting, not *self-business*. He is a tool, and you are a substance in his hand, a gemstone. You are a gemstone and he is cutting in order to reveal the Light. He must cut until the original Light emerges, until its value is fully developed. If you are a gemstone that has fallen into his hands, he must cut it to make the Light emerge. He must cut on all four sides. He must cut and polish and make you valuable. He must make you valuable and place you into a valuable treasury. He is cutting in order to place you in the treasury. That is the work he must do. Why? It is a substance that has been given into his hands. If it is given into his hands, this is what he must do.

Thus, the stone may feel pain. An Insān Kāmil will simply reveal the value of the gem. There is nothing in it for him. He will work hard to take you to the place in which you must be kept—that treasury. The moment you come to that place, you will understand. Before then, you will feel pain, the gemstone will feel the pain. When all the other bits of stone and all the other colors that are attached to it are being cut, there might be pain. That is the pain. However, if you allow him to hold you in the correct manner now, you will know the value of doing so later.

Currently, all you have to do is recite a mantra after they say, "Hand over two hundred fifty dollars." You merely have to say some words after they tell you, "Do that mantra and give us two hundred fifty dollars."

He does not do this work. A *Truth-Man* does not take from you and encourage you to keep living as a stone. Cutting is his work, so the pain will come to you. The pain will come.

He is the doctor and he must lance the boil in order to remove the pus. While he cuts, it will hurt. You should not shout, "He is cutting me!" He has to cut in order to drain out the infection. When the pus comes out, you will feel better. No matter what the disease, it must be cut away. Whether it is a tumor, a boil, or a cyst, it causes pain and must be cut. That is his work, the work of a good Guru Nādan. If we can utilize that point in each instance, we will be well.

You must stay with a Shaikh and be cut for twelve years like this. After all, it is not a little thing. Is it only a small fire? It begins right from the roots until the end where the branches, the leaves, and the flowers grow. Therefore, it must be cut. You must stay with him for twelve years in order to be cut until you are *clear*. There is no benefit in just being there. This must be understood. You must bear it. You must bear it and surrender, saying, "This is healing me."

His work is healing. You must be aware of that. You must have the faith and the certitude. "This is not to hurt me, this is to heal my illnesses. This is to remove the fire that is burning me." You must have that certitude and determination.

When we weep with our eyes, it is outwardly apparent. When we weep inside, the pain is not outwardly visible, so the world does not see it. The world only sees when we weep with our eyes. What comes out of our eyes is water. When we weep inside, blood flows. When we weep inside, the blood gushes out. When people look at us here, there is water. We must stop crying those tears of blood. That is why this remedy is required. This is what you must think about. Inside, there are tears of blood. Inside, there are blood-sucking demons. Outside, we see a small cut. Inside, your blood is all being sucked away.

The work of a Shaikh who is an Insān Kāmil is to stop that loss of blood inside.

In the work that he does, each cut will hurt. You must bear the pain. You must endeavor to bear it. You must endeavor to think. You must endeavor to comprehend. You must endeavor to understand. There will be peace in doing so, and there will be *sabūr, shukūr,* and *tawakkul,* patience, gratitude, and trust in God. If you reflect like this, there will be no pain for you. You must think, "Oh! I am in pain now because the sickness that I have is being cut—but it must be cut away, entirely cut away." You must have that certitude. "The sickness itself is hurting me more; thus, it must be removed."

If thoughts of certitude like that come to you, the pain will not harm you. Then you can be *clear, clear.*

Four hundred trillion ten thousand illnesses—those thoughts, and the fires that originate from those thoughts—must all be cut away. That is the reason it will take twelve years to cut them away. You must be a child who can bear pain. This is your sickness and he is cutting it away. You must have faith, thinking, "This is my Father and he is cutting away my sickness. He is utilizing the fire to cauterize the wounds." This is how you must be.

If you can be like this, utilizing patience like this with thoughts like this, wisdom like this, and intelligence like this, it will be easy. Then you will have no inner pain. Then each sickness can be healed. Each point will be healed. All your karma will be cut away. All your sins will be cut away. All your doubts will be cut away. All your desires will be cut away.

The moment these connections are cut away, there will be Light—God's Power. This is what he will do. "A good Guru Nādan does not kill. He does not kill, he does not kill." What he does is dispel your horrible qualities. After they are dispelled only God's Power remains—the value remains, the perfection remains. Then he can give you the crown in God's kingdom. Then he can put you into that treasury.

That is the way a Shaikh, an Insān Kāmil, a good Guru Nādan, will act. You must think of this. After thinking, you must bear it. As he cuts away each section, he cuts your opinions. When he begins to cut the opinions that you regard as golden, it will hurt as he cuts. But they are actually a sickness. That is what you must think of. As each child thinks of this, he must briefly bear the pain with a little patience. If you can bear it, the Guru will remove the tumor, he will remove the fire, and extinguish it. When the fire is extinguished, you will feel better.

If you have doubt when he cuts, it will develop into a cancer in the future. It will turn everything he does upside down. Doubt must be dispelled. You must think of this.

When doubt is dispelled, you are me. You become me, and then there is One—you and I are One.

Each child must think of this. This is the work the Guru does, that a good Guru Nādan does. It is not a business. Is it a business to cut into his own body? That is what a good Guru Nādan does.

Your body is his body. Your sickness is his. Your fire is his. That is what he is cutting. Thus, you are not two. Your sickness is now in him. Thus, he cuts. You must not see it as two. You must not see it in this way. Your sickness and your pain are in him. He is cutting himself.

You are not two. Do not think you are two. The sickness has entered him and he has to cut himself. But because you are within him, it will hurt you too. You are in pain because you hold the sickness within yourself. That is your ignorance. Think of this. How much there is that has to be cut!

THE DISCIPLE
How did we get so lucky?

The Shaikh

You must have had a connection to God before. There was a connection. Just as a seed has a connection to the earth, that point, that truth, your connection to God—that connection—grew there within you. Like a seed growing in the earth, your truth grew in that point.

It is difficult to obtain. It had to come from something you did before, or something you are doing now, or something you did in the womb. Some kind of goodness has come to you—a dot, an atom, a particle, has come. It is there. Seeing the hollow in the ground, the water has come to fill it.

Thus, the pain is ignorance. Please think. Outside, we weep water. Inside, we weep blood. Inside, the blood gushes out. This is just water. Everyone observing us sees the water that comes from weeping. But God sees the blood gushing out inside. Truth and God and the good Guru Nādan weep when they see it.

The world will weep when it sees tears, but God, the Truth, and the good Guru Nādan will weep when they see the tears of blood, and wipe them away. The place from which the blood flows must be cut off. That is his work.

Very well. Thank you. Each child, please think.

July 14, 1981
THE LOVE

You should have no doubt, suspicion, arrogance, or anger. The father's explanations, the father's words, the father's love are given equally to all children who live under his protection.

Yet your own mistakes could enter into this.

Why? He has two breasts. One breast is for giving you the milk of wisdom while the other contains the milk of worldly love to dispel your hunger, illness, and old age in the world. He has two kinds of milk to nurture you. The milk that alleviates your hunger depends on how you hold on to him, how you drink the milk, how your mouth sucks, and how you take in the milk. The milk that alleviates the hunger of your soul depends on your own mouth. It depends on how you hold on to him: whether you drink without hurting him and without hurting yourself, the way a baby drinks milk, with that kind of love.

The results will depend on your own mouth and come to you through your own effort.

It is not your father's fault. Every child, every hungry child, can come to drink. A child who is looking for that milk must search for it. Your father has two breasts. Your hunger will be alleviated according to the manner in which you drink. The hunger of your soul and your worldly hunger will both be alleviated. It depends on your own mouth and your own effort. If instead you make comparisons as you look around at what others are doing—here and there, here and there—while you merely put your mouth up to that breast, your hunger will not be alleviated. You must drink at the correct time.

If you think, "She is drinking, he is drinking, and I'm not getting any! He is developing well but nothing is coming to me," then that is the fault of your own mouth. The others are holding on, drinking and satisfying their hunger while you are just looking at the others, looking here and there, making comparisons with doubt and suspicion.

The nipple is there, so if you drink in the appropriate manner, your hunger will be alleviated. The nipple is neither bigger nor smaller for anyone. The amount that comes to you will depend on your own mouth. Your method of drinking is at fault. Your focus is at fault. Your effort is at fault. Your mouth is at fault. The fault is not in the nipple. Each nipple has three openings. There are three openings in each nipple. It depends on how you squeeze and how you hold on. Whose fault is it? It is your fault.

You must think of that state. That is how to drink milk from your father. Thus, you must make an effort to draw out the milk and drink in an appropriate way. You just need to press lightly and the milk will come.

If at times you bite, "*Avu!*" and try to force out the milk, you will get only blood. If at other times you relax your lips, open your mouth without sucking, and say, "*Ah,*" the milk will not come.

You must hold on to your father and embrace him with a correct embrace, an embrace of love, a proper embrace. If you hold on to him and drink like that, your worldly hunger will be satisfied and your soul's hunger will be satisfied. It depends on your own effort, your own care, your own love. You must discover how to drink. It is your own responsibility to search for the wisdom, to drink the milk of wisdom, and also to drink the milk that belongs to your worldly life.

If you do not do this, it is your own fault. If you have arrogance and differences, your own faults will harm you.

One child drinks carefully and develops well. The milk comes, that child is doing his work and growing. If you make comparisons, looking at the children over here and over there, if you develop doubt, arrogance, and that which is known as the "I," you will not drink. Then you are nurturing neither your life nor your wisdom. You are drinking neither the milk of wisdom nor the milk of life. That is your fault.

These are the two nipples that belong to your father: one for proceeding on the path of your soul, one for proceeding on the path to God. The two nipples are offered with equality for your life. Your father has equality. You must understand this.

If you think, "She is getting more. I am getting nothing like that. I am not developing. She is progressing well, but I am not succeeding. Thus, there is no place for me here," that will be your own placeless quality, your own embrace-less quality, your own not-knowing-how-to-drink quality. You are making comparisons and looking at others.

He who drinks, drinks by himself with care. That is how he progresses. You must reflect upon this. Your doubt displays only separation. It does not satisfy your wisdom's hunger, your soul's hunger, your life's hunger, or your worldly hunger. You will suffer. Whose fault is this? It is each individual's own fault.

You are all siblings who have been born under the protection of the same father. There is a tree that has good fruit. It bears good, ripe fruit. You need to find it. There is good fruit with good taste and good color. You need to eat that fruit.

However, do not stand under the tree throwing stones and saying, "It has fruit!" The fruits will not fall if you throw stones at them. Even if some do fall, they will be damaged. They will fall to the ground, damaged. Thus, you must try to climb the tree.

What must you do in the endeavor to climb? You must first observe the tree a little. Is it a tree with thorns or is it a good tree? Are there branches on which to climb? You must look for these things.

Having observed the tree in this manner, you must hold the tree in an embrace. You must climb by embracing it. After you climb up, you can remain in the state in which you should live and then pick the fruit and eat it. That will satisfy your hunger.

Thus, if you say, "One child is acting in one way, another child is acting in another way. I have no place here. They have a certain way of acting. I have a different way. They are not showing me love," you have not picked the fruit.

Your own heart must hold on to your brothers and sisters. Your own love must hold on to them. Your father has the fruit. Just as you embrace the tree in order to eat the fruit, your own love must embrace and hold on to each child in the tree. After you embrace and hold on to them, you must climb into that love. You can pick the fruit only if you climb.

Your own heart will show you your own differences, saying, "You are not embracing with love. You are not embracing and holding on to others."

If you do not embrace and hold on, the tree will say nothing and the fruits will always be above you. Thus, your hearts must go to embrace each of your brothers and sisters. You must embrace and hold on to them. You will be able to eat beautiful fruits if you embrace and hold on to your siblings with your hands and your love.

Those fruits will be flawless.

If you merely stand under the tree throwing stones at one thing or another, anything that happens to fall from the tree will be damaged. You will never find unity in your life like that. Only your doubt will grow. The ripening fruits will not. The unity will not grow, the love will not grow, the happiness will not develop, and you will not succeed. This is what some of you experienced in your lives when you yourselves did not show love.

Let's put a small fish on a hook. A fisherman will make it move in the proper way. Only then will the next fish come to catch it. If the fisherman does not move the bait and it stands as rigid and still as the hook, the fish will not come. If the impaled fish is stiff and motionless, the next fish will not come. The fisherman must make it wiggle. The baitfish must move. That is the reason the next fish will come to catch it. That is how the larger fish will come to catch the smaller one.

Your love must bear fruit like this and actually move. If it moves, another love will come to catch it, even if it has to die in the process. It will come to catch it, even if it is about to die. It will come to catch it, even if it is in danger. You must think of this. Other hearts will not come to catch you if you do not generate love in your own heart, if you do not move and bow down to greet them, if you do not open your own heart. However, if you keep your own heart open, others will come to it. Others will also come with open hearts.

Each of you, make your own heart *clear*. Show your love. Show your unity and peace. When you demonstrate the compassion of your just deeds, that practice will make you exalted.

If that does not exist within you, if instead you have the arrogance known as "I" and doubt, it will harm you and kill you. It will separate you.

It will separate you from God.

It will separate you from truth. It will separate you from compassion. It will separate you from unity. It will separate you from Allāh. It will separate you from the correct wisdom in your life. It will separate you from the love that melts and dissolves. It will separate you from the good things and then you will receive the fiery things.

Then you will be seized by and united with sins such as anger, haste, impatience, jealousy, treachery, pride, falsehood, theft, and murder. Then your life will be hell while you are still alive, and you will also go to hell when you die. You will be the one generating this state.

If you open your heart, immerse yourself in God's compassion, and demonstrate His compassion—demonstrating that God is love, that good works are most exalted, and that compassion is the most beloved thing in your life—if you display His compassionate qualities, then the ripening love will be generated there in your open heart. Grace will be generated. Wealth will be generated. *Rahmah*[10] will be generated. Beauty will be generated. Light will be generated. The fruit that never perishes will be formed there. Undiminishing treasures will be generated. A long life will be generated. God's grace and His treasures will be made complete there. Unity will be generated. The understanding that all lives are your own life will be generated.

In this, you can get peace. You must think of this.

However, if you lock your *qalb*, your innermost heart, and the

---

10 *rahmah*   the grace of compassion and mercy

One who is Love comes to knock on the door, He will say, "It is locked," and He will leave. If wealth comes to visit you, it will say, "*Oho*! It is locked. The house is dark," and it will leave. Even if the grace of God itself comes, it will say, "*Tch*! This is a deserted house," and it will leave. Regardless of how much love others come with to see you, they will not be able to do anything with a locked house, and they will leave.

If you keep your heart locked like this, nothing can ever enter it, can it? Thus, you must keep your *qalbs* open. It is only through keeping them open that you can obtain the benefit, reach the truth, reach peace, attain serenity, and experience tranquility in your life. You can attain tranquility. You must think of this.

If you do not think of this, your doubt, your jealousy, your arrogance, and your suspicions will consume you, separate you from truth, and isolate you. They will separate you from God, truth, and wisdom, while plucking you out of your exalted life and manifesting degradation.

You must realize and understand this with certainty. You must know how much sweetness there is in the milk you drink from your father and the unity of living as one group of children under the protection of one father.

Your stomach will not be filled if there are faults in the mouth with which you drink, if you make comparisons, if you do not hold on to him while you drink, or if you look around at the countryside. The milk will not come to you if you look here and there instead of embracing him and drinking the milk with love. You must gently squeeze and draw it in, gently place your lips on that nipple, and pump it out.

Children, jeweled lights of my eyes, when you travel in a car, there is a horn. In the past, we squeezed the horn. The air inside the rubber bulb was squeezed out, and the air outside then filled it. The horn was pumped. When we pumped it gently, the sound, "*ouuu*," went out. The air that went out "*bom*," then pulled in the new air. On the roads upon which we traveled, when we needed, we could squeeze the horn a little. The "*ouuu*" sound went out, and when we released it, the horn drew the air back in.

Similarly, you must drink from the nipple with your good

conduct, your love, your good manners, and purity of heart. You must show love like this and drink. If you embrace and hold on to that breast in the correct way, with the correct conduct, it will give you what it has, and it will draw in the air that you have. It will draw in your karma, your sins, and your doubts, incinerate them, and give you its own sound. The horn will give you the "*ouuu*" sound that is within it and alleviate your hunger. That sound will warn you and also show you the beauty.

The milk that the father gives is similar. You must place your mouth on that nipple with good conduct, with reverence, with love, and with good manners while you embrace him, hold on to him, and drink. You must be actively involved in the process. You must not make comparisons or look here and there. You must endeavor to drink until your hunger is appeased.

If you fail to do this with love, and if you look here and there instead—biting him at one time, crushing him at another time, lying there, looking around, and kicking him at another time—you will not be able to drink if you act like that.

The child that drinks will grow. The child that does not drink will fail to thrive. His body will weaken and his strength will decrease. It is your doubt that tells you, "He is different and I am different." This is your mistake. Your own nature makes the mistake for you. Your own qualities and your own heart make the mistakes. You must think of this. It is your mind.

You need to think of how to embrace him and how to act. You need to think of how to embrace him, how to drink the milk, and how to have unity. You need to think of how we should embrace each other and live together in unity. How should we live with our father? How should we embrace our brothers and sisters? How should we embrace and hold on to the truth and satisfy our hunger? You must know the correct way to do this.

Only then will you reach serenity and peace in your life, and attain victory in your worldly life and in the life of your soul. You will attain well-being in your inner life and in your outer life. You will find happiness in both joy and sorrow. You will be able to attain the victory with your brothers and sisters in your life in the *ākhirah*, the kingdom of God, and in your life in the *dunyā*, the world, and obtain His *rahmah*. You must think of this. Please think of this. Do you understand?

If you live in the state in which it is possible to think of this, if you possess the code of conduct through which it is possible to understand this code of conduct, if you understand and act accordingly, you will not be angry with one another, you will not criticize one another, you will not attack one another, you will not act with treachery towards one another.

The fragrance of a flower does not come from the outside. The fragrance of a flower exists in the flower. Only when the flower opens does the fragrance come from it. If the flower does not open, the fragrance will not emerge. We can see this, can we not? If the flower is closed, can we see its beauty? No. The colors are revealed only when it is open. Is the fragrance there when the flower is closed? No. The fragrance emerges only when the flower opens. The fragrance comes from it when the flower blooms.

Similarly, if you keep your hearts closed, the beauty will never come to you. You will be closed. If you are rolled shut, the beauty will not come, the fragrance will not come. The fragrance comes from a flower when it unfurls. Thus, if you keep your *qalbs* rolled shut, the beauty and the bliss will not come to you. Only if that *bū*, that flower, that *qalb-bū*, the flower of your innermost heart, blooms, only if it unfurls will the fragrance of grace, the fragrance of *gnānam*, divine wisdom, the fragrance of the soul, and the fragrance of Allāh's *rahmah* that exists within it emanate from it. The blossoming flower is there in your *qalb*. Its beauty will come, its fragrance will come, its qualities will come, and its happiness will come.

If you unfurl your *qalbs*, then everyone with the nose that loves that fragrance will take in the fragrance from your *qalbs*. "Ah, beautiful! Such a good fragrance, a blissful fragrance," they will say. It will come to the hearts of all who have the nose, all who have the wisdom, and they will all come to embrace you. They will endeavor to touch it in order to take in the smell, will they not? If your *qalb-bū* is like that, then the love within others will come looking for it, and they will join you. They will take in the fragrance and they will experience the bliss when they see its beauty. Each one of you must make that blossom in your heart correct. That is the flower garden.

You must not think that the flower garden exists elsewhere.

They say, "In heaven there are flower gardens, groves of fruit trees, a river of honey, a river of precious nectar, a river of milk," but there are no such places and rivers there. They say, "There are swings, there are swinging beds, there are lovely houses in heaven," and so forth, but none of those things will ever be elsewhere. All the houses, all the flower gardens, all the blossoms, all the fruit trees, the seventy thousand tastes in each ripening fruit, the seventy thousand fragrances in each flower are all in your heart.

Only here.

The river of milk, the river of honey, the river of precious nectar, and the exquisite beauty that is called the river of grace are all in your heart. The *flower-heart* is here. Your *qalb* is the flower garden. This is the house of absolute purity, the house of heaven. This is the kingdom of heaven for you, the kingdom of your Father. It is here. This is your prayer mat, the place for prayer. The flower garden of your life is here.

Your qualities are a flower garden for you. Your actions are a fruit orchard for you. Your duty, service, and love are the seventy thousand ripening tastes within them. Your loving qualities are the sweetness within them. Your duties are the *houris*, the children who will serve you, there. All the duties, deeds, and service you do for God, all of them, will take form and become your *houris*. The prayers you perform will become the *malā'ikah*, the angels, that serve you.

Your house there is being constructed of the things you seek here. The wealth you get there will result from the work you do here. There you will receive the wealth of grace, the wealth of the *ākhirah*, the wealth of *'ilm*, divine knowledge, and the *rahmah*.

The peace and serenity you get there will come from the worship and the prayers you perform here. How you act here will become for you a kingdom of heaven, a heavenly flower garden, a fruit orchard. Each good thought will become a precious gem. When the beauty of what you do with a completely open heart, a completely open *qalb*, a completely open beauty, comes into being within you, that will become the beautiful wealth of the *ākhirah* for you. These will be your ornaments.

Everything you will get there is being formed here. This is the heaven you will get there. This is what you will carry with you if you want to abide there. You must drink here from this fruit orchard, this flower garden, this river of milk, this river of honey, this river of grace, and reach bliss. If you can make each of your qualities into an individual fruit as you build this house, perform the duties, the prayers, and the worship, these will be the fruits that never perish, the beauty that never diminishes.

The fragrances of that flower exist here. The honey is here. The grace is here. The milk is here—the milk of love, the milk of grace. They must melt and dissolve. This house is your heaven.

Your Father will give you the deed to the house to take with you.

If you do not build that house here, if you do not plant the fruit trees and the flower garden here, you will not develop those flavors, that beauty, or those sweet tastes.

This is the primary principle in your duty and in your birth. Allāh's Ka'bah is here. Allāh's house is here. Allāh's place of prayer is here. Allāh's judgment is here. Allāh's kingdom is here.

You must run this absolutely pure kingdom correctly. Allāh's kingdom must be run by Allāh with His qualities, His blessings, His actions, His deeds, *sabūr*, *shukūr*, *tawakkul*, and *al-hamdu lillāh*, patience, gratitude, trust, and giving praise only to God. His three thousand divine qualities, His ninety-nine actions, duties, and tasks are our *wilāyāt*, our miracles.

The *wilāyah* is to search for ourselves within ourselves.

Those who embrace this beauty and bliss within themselves are called *mu'minūn*, believers. Those who have received the Light of Allāh, those who are without blemish, those who are without fault, those who are without bigotry, those who are without prejudice, those who have reached peace, those who have experienced the peace of treating all lives as their own, those who bring peace to all lives, those who give love to all lives, those who embrace and hold on to all lives and ease their suffering and problems are the believers.

Until you find this compassion and love, until you build that house within your *qalb*, until you understand the fruit orchard, until you understand the river of milk from which you must drink in order to quench your thirst, until you understand the river of honey that is the *'ilm*, until you understand the river of grace and attain bliss there, until you stand within the qualities, the peace, the tranquility, and the unity known as Allāh's treasures and act accordingly, until you are aware that all lives are your own life and serve them accordingly, until you perform these duties, your duties will be the duties of hell.

Those who do not build this house will build the house of hell.

The *nafs ammārah*, the desires, of the *dunyā*, the illusory magic tricks of the *dunyā*, the magic tricks performed through mantras, the legerdemain, the conjuring arts of maya, the arrogance, the karma, the betrayal, the treachery, the deceit, the jealousy, the anger, the separation known as "I and you," the bigotry, the backbiting, the telling of lies, pride, garnering praise for oneself, acting with the actions of the "I," speaking abusively, spreading lies between people, spreading slander, and taking vengeance are the house of hell.

That will be the house of hell here for your life, it will be the house of hell for you after you die, and it will be the house of hell in the *qabr*, the grave. Your life will be the house of *adhāb*, punishment. You will then have to accept the *adhāb* of a life without peace. If you build that house, if you build the house of the hellfire known as *huwah*, the chasm of fire, you will burn in the *dunyā* and in that fire. That will be your suffering.

The fire you set here to punish others will become your house in hell. What you laugh at and weep for here will become your house of hell. What you call joy and sorrow here will be the house of the hell of your aspirations. The house of hell is reserved and designated for you through your own intentions.

You are building the house of hell with the scorpions that you have reserved and designated for yourself. Thus you yourself are building the suffering, the sorrow, and the sin. From that, the extreme pain, the fire known as *jahannam*, the deepest hell, will come to you in the *dunyā* and in the *ākhirah*, and become the state you reach in your *qalb* and in your life.

It is easy to talk about all of this, but only if you open your *qalb* and analyze what is there will you genuinely understand. No benefit will come from talk. You must actually discover how to open the house of your *qalb* and make it good. You must do your research with wisdom and plant your crops. You must build your beautiful house. You must build the house of grace as the house of grace. You must gather the wealth of the *rahmah* as the house of the *rahmah*. You must build the house of the *mubārakāt*—the wealth of God's love in all three worlds—for the world of the soul, for the world of the *dunyā*, and for the world of the *ākhirah*.

When you gather the materials for the house of the *mubārakāt* that is the *qudrah*, the power of God, and the treasures that comprise Allāh's *rahmah*, you will be among those who will eternally possess inexhaustible wealth, you will be among those who have received eternal *hayāh*, life, without death, you will be among those who have received bliss without any suffering, you will be among those who lead long lives without suffering or sorrow.

You and Allāh will be eternally together. You will live in your Father's house and your Father will live in your house. Such will be the *firdaus*, the paradise, of your life. That *firdaus-paradise* will be the state of the house of the heaven you have built.

You must search for the *'ilm* and the qualities commensurate with it through your Father. You can obtain this wealth from a Father who is a man of wisdom, a Father with *'ilm*, a Father with good qualities. Then you can receive that exalted state and that wealth for your life.

Precious brothers and sisters, precious jeweled lights of my eyes, you are the children to whom I have given birth. From now on, each child must reflect upon the efforts he is making. You must think of what these treasures are.

If you release a drop of water onto the ground, it will sink into it. The drop of water will sink into the ground and soften it. If you then dig down to the aquifer, it can give you many drops of water. There will be many drops of water able to quench the thirst of many people.

Similarly, even if you do only one duty for the sake of Allāh to the extent that you can, the eyes of many springs will open within you as you continue. They will be the eyes of the springs of His grace.

Your duty, the prayers you perform, the charity you give, the donations you give, the love you give, all your embraces, and all that you learn will amount to a single drop. If you keep releasing and releasing each drop of water to loosen the ground, digging until you reach the spring of grace, the spring of Allāh's qualities will begin to bubble up. When that spring bubbles up and comes to you, you will be able to experience so many drops of water because of the individual drops you poured onto that ground.

If you give one word to Allāh, how many discourses of grace you will be able to hear! Your efforts are all just single drops. If you keep on making the effort to go towards Him and if you discover that spring, your claim to it will bring you so much. Then you can intermingle with it and other lives can intermingle with it. Then the spring that brings peace to everyone will flow, will it not? When that spring of grace, that spring of Light, that spring of *'ilm*, that spring of good qualities, bubbles up, it will make everyone peaceful.

As you release each drop of effort and make it your own, those single drops will begin to soften the ground. As you keep digging while focusing on the signs, as you struggle, as you keep making the effort, putting your love into it and wetting the ground, melting it and dissolving it, digging into it, many springs will appear and the wealth of Allāh's grace will come to you and bring you peace. It will alleviate everyone's hunger and sin. It will extinguish the karma, the arrogance, and the errors. Past evil and future evil will all be dispelled. As it bubbles up, it will keep increasing and satisfy all hunger: the hunger of the soul, the hunger of the world, and the hunger of the *ākhirah*. Do this.

However, when you release that drop, you must never think, "I did it! You did it! I gave a drop! I gave this! I gave that!"

No matter what you do, it will barely amount to a drop. It will not be equal to one drop. However God pours and pours down His blessings with great abundance and makes them constantly increase. This is His wealth. He does not say, "I."

Even if you release a drop, a drop of prayer, to Him, even if you do genuinely pray, it will not be equal to one drop of His melting. Even if you genuinely search for Him, it will not compare to one drop of His love. Even all that you genuinely do will not compare to one drop of what He does. It is a mistake to say, "I, I did that."

In His state, what He does will multiply. What He increases is the increase. You must think of how many times He multiplies it. Think of this and forget the "I."

In any kind of worship you perform, you must surrender and place your *tawakkul*, your trust, in Allāh, saying, "*Al-hamdu lillāh*, all praise belongs to God." Say, "*Al-hamdu lillāh*," while you do it. Say, "*Al-hamdu lillāh*," while you walk. No matter what you do, place it in His responsibility and say, "*Al-hamdu lillāh. Tawakkul-'alAllāh. Allāh.*" Do this. When you do your duty in this way, opening the eye of that spring, obtaining that *rahmah*, abundantly giving it to the people, giving it to all lives, giving it to all who have been born with you, serving them with that great abundance, and feeding it to them until their *qalbs* are full of grace—on that day you will become His children.

He will be in your house and you will be in His house. That is the house of the *Rahmatul-'ālamīn*, the Mercy of All the Universes. *Al-hamdu lillāh.* Think of this.

Think of this and open your *qalbs*. Plant the flower garden there. Plant the orchard there. Start the farm there. Build the house there. Bring the kingdom of Allāh into being there. Struggle hard to bring those things into being and obtain the *rahmah*.

You must not think of religions, ethnic groups, or scriptures. There is only one place for Allāh.

There are two kinds of wealth: you can can drink in the victory of your *hayāh*, your life, and the victory of His *rahmah*. The nipple will exist in the *qalb* of a genuine Insān Kāmil, a Perfected Human Being. Find it and drink from it. You will drink and reach peace according to your own effort. That is the heaven you will find, and the treasures within it.

As-salāmu 'alaikum wa rahmatullāhi wa barakātuhu. Peace and the compassionate grace and blessings of God be upon you. *Āmīn.*

June 30, 1981
The Difficulties

An ordinary guru will stand as a pillar in hell. He will stand as a pillar in hell and he will subject you to hell. He will be a pillar in hell and you will be the people for hell. That is what an ordinary guru or shaikh will do as he leads his life. Such a guru will have a guru title and position, good food, name, fame, and a good *self-business* to run. You can easily obtain and follow such a guru.

However, it is difficult to obtain a Gnāna Guru, a Gnāna Shaikh. If there is such a Shaikh, it will be extremely difficult to establish a connection between you and him. Before this connection can be established, he has to cut away all your qualities, the sixty-four sexual games, the sixty-four arts and sciences, and the four hundred trillion ten thousand *spiritual* qualities. No matter where you turn, he will cut away everything. No matter in which direction you walk, he will cut away everything. He will cut away everything you bring to him. He will cut away all the words you sing. He will cut away all the roads on which you travel. Therefore, it will be difficult to be with him.

He will cut away every thought that comes to you. He will cut away everything you look at. He will block all the paths you traverse, all the paths you love. He will block all the paths on which you intend to move. He will block all the paths belonging to desire. He will block all paths. That is why it is difficult. Then he will take you on his path. He will open only that one path and show it to you. He will cut away all the other paths.

You may love to ride horses. He will say, "If you ride that horse, you will fall. Climb onto your own horse. The other horse will throw you off. There is a horse within you—the *vāsi kudiray*, the horse of the breath. Climb onto that. Ride that. Do not look at the world. Look at yourself. Do not find fault with the world. Look at yourself, see with your own wisdom what your body is doing, and find fault with it. Do not be angry at the world. Be angry at yourself after you discover the faults within yourself. Do not analyze worldly life. Your own life is an immense world and that life is within you. Endeavor to think about that.

"Do not go around lecturing the world. There are many lectures within you. The lectures within you have existed since the time you were born and will exist until your end.

"Do not go around reading about the world in worldly books. There is a book within you, a history book of four hundred trillion ten thousand births. Read that history book. That is a continuous history that goes from the *awwal* to the *ākhirah*, from creation to the kingdom of God.

"That history is an unwritten history. It has to come from your own focus. The writing must be revealed through the focus of wisdom. The writing in the book within you is water-writing. If you simply look at the book, you will not see it. The book must be heated. The writing will be visible only after it is heated. It is water-writing—earth, fire, water, air, and ether water-writing. It is written with water.

"You must place a heat source there. You must place the heat known as wisdom there and then look at it. You must hold the heat known as wisdom in the Resplendence known as Allāh up to your soul. Then you will see the text. If you hold it up and read like that, you will understand the eons and the conditions that existed throughout the two hundred million years when the water, the fire, the air, the earth, and each creation were created. There are so many lessons of this nature to be learned in that life.

"You say you are praying and worshiping. You are doing

everything the world does. But look at what God is doing. Then you will understand how He worships, how He does the *toluhay*, the formal prayers, how He prays, how He performs *'ibādah*, service, how He does duty, how He is an *'abd*, a Slave, how He is a Servant, how He is great, how He is small, how He is perfect, how He is poor, how He lives without a place, how He lives with a place. You must perform this historical analysis within yourself and understand it.

"Then you will understand and learn how to pray, how to perform the *toluhay*, and how to do the *'ibādah*. Holding up the heat of your wisdom in the Light known as Allāh—in the Resplendence—look at your book, look at your *qalb*, your innermost heart.

"Then when you look, you will understand what is evil, what is good, what is unjust, what is coming to kill you, what is coming to eat you, what is coming to enslave you, what is already enslaving you, what is ruling you, what is turning you upside down, and what is killing you.

"Look at your illnesses. These are the illnesses. To heal the illnesses, you must read this history. You must study only this history. This is the time for it. The lessons you need to learn every second and every minute are here."

The reason the Shaikh blocks all the other paths is so you do not become involved in looking at this, looking at that, looking at this. "Do not go there!" he says. "They are all illnesses that will kill you. They are all illnesses that will utterly destroy you. They are all illnesses that will mesmerize you. You will alternate between waking, sleeping, dying, and then sleeping again. You will alternate between being unconscious, waking, falling, walking, crying, laughing, and moaning. You will do all those things. Those other paths are all illnesses that have come to kill you.

"Unable to carry what you once loved, what you once desired, what you once carried in the past, you will have to put those things down and cry. What you followed in the past will leave you—it will stay with you for a little while and then abandon you in the jungle as prey for the animals that live there. You will sail the ocean somewhere for a little while, your mind will operate the boat for a little while, and then leave you boat-less in the middle of the ocean to become prey to the fish, the sharks, and the currents. All the paths you construct with your thoughts are fatal illnesses. This is not it."

As you proceed, you will say, "The light is there! The *gnānam* is there! The guru is there! The perfection is there! Heaven is there! Gold is there, and silver! There is a place for me! There is a palace for me!" But they are all merely dreams that are actual illnesses.

Soon those dreams will all depart and you will be abandoned mid-journey and delivered to maya, currents, magnets, desire, attachment, religion, ethnic groups, *shaitān*, hell, worms, and insects. Your own mind and intellect will take you there and abandon you. Then you will suffer.

Thus, you must study the countless lessons of the countless worlds within you with a *clear* understanding. You must study the lessons of the eighteen thousand universes, *'ālamul-arwāh*, the *awwal*, the *dunyā*, and the *ākhirah*—the world of pure souls, the creation, this world, and the kingdom of God. Because you must study them during your lifetime, a Gnāna Shaikh will instruct you to read this inner history book as he blocks everything else you think of, as he blocks everything else you intend to do.

It is in this situation that the difficulties between you and what he says will arise. You can live with him only if you always endeavor to give up what you want and accept what he wants.

That is the reason the majority will not stay with the Gnāna Shaikh. Not one of the majority will ever be with him. Nor will he normally have very many children. He will not have very many disciples. For him to have one or two or three or four or ten or twenty would be a multitude. The majority will not stay with him. Those who do stay will be in the minority. If he were to get fifteen or twenty, they would be the leaders of the eighteen thousand universes. They would be the first rank in the kingdom of God. They would be those who have received the wealth of God. That is the reason you must learn these lessons.

Everything he tells you will hurt you. It will hurt your thoughts. It will hurt your *qalb*. It will hurt all your thoughts, desires, attachments, and plans. It will bring anguish to your mind. It will bring anguish to your intellect. You will leave him because of your suffering and anger. You will fly away. There are countless people who have run like this. They gather together and then they all run away. They come to unite and then they all go their separate ways.

Therefore, we who remain and hold on are just a few children. The little Funny Family of God's Ants is just a small family, God's Family. There are hardly any of them. Most of them have run away. Only those who entirely and absolutely respect the roadblock of what the Shaikh says will remain.

The others will all be market groups: those who gather in the marketplace, the guru-business marketplace, the shaikh-business, the religion-business, the ethnic group-business marketplace. All of them will gather in the assembly of the *self-business* market. They will all come to the marketplace to obtain *gnānam*, to obtain miracles, and to obtain liberation. Oh! There will be multitudes and multitudes.

When you look, at the end there will only be one or two with that Shaikh. The rest will not be with him. The rest will again pick up the things they came with and go back to where they came from. They will all come to the marketplace. They will gather at the market, saying, "We will study *gnānam*. We will perform miracles. We will reach God. We will reach heaven." They will assemble there.

If a genuine Insān Kāmil Shaikh should fall into your hands, he will block all your thoughts. Thus, you will avoid him and run away. He will block all your intentions, so you will run. He will block all your desires. He will block all your ways of life. He will block everything you bring him. He will show you only one path. He will block all other paths. He will show you only one treasure. He will block all other treasures. He will show you only the path belonging to one *ānmā*, one soul. He will cut away all the other souls. He will show you only one life. He will cut away all the other lives. Thus, it will be difficult to stay with him and to hold on. Everyone will leave and go elsewhere. All of them will scatter, run away, and leave.

This is the difficult path of an Insān Kāmil, the difficult education, the difficult research, the life-research, that will be *clearly* evident only within yourself—your own history. That is the reason this section is few, and that the other section, the assembly at the marketplace, has *self-business*. They will leave.

They will go to a guru who shows them how to act the way they want to act. Those gurus will live exactly how they want to live and engage in *self-business*, and they will allow you to also enter into the *self-business* section. It suits them. It suits all of them.

If there is a dog that wishes to eat feces and if there is a feces-eating guru, they will get together. If there is a cow that wants to eat grass, there will be a grass-eating guru to milk it. Like this, every thought you have that suits them will be fine. It will be a suitable match. If you want to be a prostitute and if he is also a prostitute, then it will be fine. If you want to be a thief and if he is also a thief, that will be all right. If the counterpart for your countless thoughts is there, you will go and bury yourself in it. That is what could become of your wisdom in the end.

If he is a genuine Shaikh, he will block everything you have and difficulties will arise for you. He will block all your thoughts and your life. He will show you only one path. Because of that, difficulties will arise. "What is this? He is crazy! He doesn't let me go there and he doesn't let me go here. He doesn't let me go to the market. He doesn't let me go to the bathroom. He doesn't let me go to sleep. What is this? He is crazy! He is crazy!" they will say and no one will stay with him.

Only four or five will remain, holding on and staying with him. They will be the rulers of the kingdom of heaven. They will be the rulers of the kingdom of the world and the kingdom of God. They will be the leaders of all love. That is the difficulty. Such a Shaikh and such a disciple will have only that one point and they will stay in that place. They will not go to the market.

All who come to the marketplace
will again seek their own villages and return to them at sunset.

As soon as the sun sets, they will all leave. Why? Each person will have bought what he was thinking of. Only one section in the marketplace will stay in that one place, with the Shaikh. They will remain on that one point. They will remain in his *qalb*. They will remain in his wisdom. They will remain in his affection. They will remain in his love. Those who remain in that compassionate love will be the minority.

Those who leave and separate from him to buy things such as miracles, other opinions, advice, and things that thieves and clowns buy, will be in the majority. They will leave him and go to the market.

They will come to the market, buy things, and then each one of them will go back to his own home. They will go back to the place known as karma. This is a point concerning the sixteen kinds of gurus in the world.

Should you find that Shaikh and go to that one place, everything you bring with you will be blocked. The entire world you carry will be blocked. The sixty-four sexual games will be blocked. The sixty-four arts and sciences will be blocked. The religions and ethnic groups will be blocked. He will block your desires. He will block your attachments. He will block your bonds. He will block the colors. He will block everything.

Only one path will be open. This path will connect the East with the West. Everything you see other than this will be blocked. Each intersection will be blocked. "Do not turn back to look at that intersection, it is blocked," he will tell you. "Do not turn back to look at this intersection either. There are groups gathered at this intersection. It is blocked. Go straight." These are the difficulties that arise between an Insān Kāmil and the disciples.

Īmān, certitude, determination, faith in the Guru, faith in the Shaikh, faith in Allāh, and faith in the *rusul*,[11] must exist. If you have that faith, certitude, determination, and *īmān*, you can follow him without failing. You can hold on to his sarong where it tucks in at the back and you can follow him in a line. If you break through the roadblocks, you will go astray. At that point he will guide you back to the path you prefer and leave you there. You will follow it and perish.

For this truth, everything else will be blocked. Suffering will come to you. Difficulty will come. Everything will appear to be difficult, but if you cut through what seems to be difficult, you will see it as a happy thing. As you continue to cut your way through it, you will see that it is happy. It will arrive as a difficulty to your mind, but as you continue to cut through it, you will see it as a happy thing.

If you run away, saying it is difficult, this will be the illness that will kill you, the illness that will enslave you in the end. You will die from this illness. It will kill you day by day. If you cut through the difficulty with certitude, you will grow day by day until you reach

---

11 *rusul,* (sing.) *rasūl*   messenger(s)

perfect completion. This is what you must understand.

This is why the Ant-Man tells you one word: study.

Learn like this. It will be very hard to stay with the Ant-Man. There will be much difficulty. All your thoughts will be difficult. All your intentions will be difficult—they will all be blocked. That is why the Ant-Man Society will not grow very much. It is extremely difficult, thus, it will not grow.

They will just run and run. They will say, "I came to learn *gnānam*," and run. They will say, "I came to get miracles," and run. After they get what they came for, they run. That is the difficulty.

Know this and stand with certitude. Live with certitude. Then like a cowboy that watches over a thousand grazing cattle, you will be able to control the grazing world within you and reach perfect completion. You will be able to reach a state of watching over the grazing cattle and goats. If you stay and hold on, the grace that will enable you to control and rule over everything in the eighteen thousand universes will come.

You must stay and hold on. You must have certitude, determination, *īmān*, faith in the Guru, faith in the Shaikh, faith in Allāh, faith in the *rusul*. If you strengthen your *īmān*, becoming *'ibād*, slaves, being transformed into his children, and proceeding with the Guru on that path, he will block all the intersections on the path that he travels. He will block them point by point and guide you. Then you can find the victory. You can find the perfection. You can find the completion. You can find the peace. You can find the tranquility. You can find the serenity in your life. That is serenity.

This must be understood.

My love you, my children, my daughters, and my sons. *My love you*, children who are the love of my *qalb*. This is the truth.

On this path, so much will be blocked. Yet you must do it. If you do not, neither you nor the Shaikh will find peace. He will not be able to finish the work he came to do and you will not be able to finish the work you came to do. It has to come to a peaceful conclusion. This is the way. This is the reason the difficulties will arise.

You must stand fast and hold on. It is your responsibility to stand fast and hold on. Then you will see. *Āmīn*.

November 17, 1982
THE DANGERS

The hand of faith and love is a good hand, a very good hand. However, people often let go of this hand. At first they hold on, but then they let go of it.

That hand does not let go.

This child let go and a lot of difficulty came to her. The hand of love spoke many words of comfort to her, told her what was happening and what was going to happen. It told her what had happened in the past and what would happen in the future. The hand of love told her everything, but she let go of it. She let go. That is how the difficulties came to her life. She made false promises and told all kinds of lies. Now her life is difficult.

The hand of love did not let go of her—her hand is the one that let go. That is why her life is difficult.

The hand of love is a very good hand. If you have done something wrong, the wisdom of that hand will hit you a little and its love will embrace you. The wisdom will hit you and the love will embrace you. When the blow comes from wisdom, it will hurt the error without hurting the love. It may hurt the ignorance, but it will never hurt wisdom and love. The ignorance will be hurt. That is how children are corrected and prevented from making mistakes so they can go on the right path. That is what love does.

The blow does not come from a stick. When his beloved child does something wrong, the Shaikh watches for a long time and then hits him with the cane known as wisdom to drive out the ignorance and lack of wisdom. Those who are ignorant and lacking in wisdom will feel the pain of the stick and some of them will leave in ignorance. They will leave. They will not have the hand of proper love and faith. Their love and faith are not sufficiently strong. They may let go of their grip at any time. They may let go at some time.

If their love and faith are sufficiently strong and if they are holding on to it in their heart, they will not let go. Then it will not hurt when their faults are hit with wisdom. They will nod and nod their heads as they listen and they will immediately think, "From now on, I will not do that." They will reflect upon what was said and hold on. They will hold on even tighter. They will hold on ever tighter.

When a mother hen pecks and pecks at her chicks, they take refuge under her belly. They burrow and burrow into her feathers and seek protection there.

As they run about, an eagle will come. If they run too far, the eagle will strike them and carry them off. If an eagle comes, there is danger. The mother hen allows her chicks to run and play and do everything else, but when the enemy arrives she will make the sound, "*Kek, kekku, kek! Kek, kekku, kek, kekku, kek!*" and they will all run towards her. They must come to burrow into her feathers. Only then can she protect them.

The chicks climb on her, peck at her head and her body, but none of that will hurt her. They jump on her, but that will not hurt her. When the enemy approaches to strike her children, the moment she knows that danger is coming, she looks around frantically, calling and calling to them, "Come! Come! Come!" If they do not respond, she pecks them. She will peck them at that time.

A father of genuine love, a father of wisdom—if you have one—will be like this. If there is an error that is about to occur in your life, he will make this sound, "*Kek, kek, kek, kek!*" If the children do not come to him at that time, he will peck them. A father of genuine love will protect his children just as a mother hen protects her chicks. His nature is to protect you from the evils of the world, from maya, from desires, from wrongdoing, and from the poison of life. A wise father of love protects you like this from the dangers approaching you.

If you leave angrily because of this, and if you let go, it is fine, but the dangers will attack you and then that will be the suffering you will undergo. Your father calls you, "*Kek, kek, kek, kek!*" The eagle has come to kill you, therefore, when he says, "*Kek, kek!*" you must go to him. It is flying up above and watching in order to catch you. It is then that your father will peck you. If you run away from him in order to escape from the peck, the eagle will strike you.

This is how a wise father of love raises his child. This is how he protects that child from the accidents of the world, from the five senses, from maya, and from the dangers that are coming into his life. At that time he will peck you or hit you with wisdom.

If you let go, those dangers will come to you. It will not be his fault. If your grip lacks faith and love, he will peck you once. If you leave to go to something else, he will feel sad, and he may either lightly or forcefully peck you at that time. If you persist in letting go, he will leave you. That will be a time of danger. The danger will seize you.

These are important and true words. It is not his fault.

A child who holds on correctly will burrow into the Shaikh like a chick burrows into the mother hen as she pecks and pecks. You can escape from the evils of life if you burrow ever more deeply into him and become more and more aware. That is how true faith and love hold the heart. That love and faith will gently stroke the child.

Another child might also have love, but it will be an ordinary love and an ordinary faith. Such a child will let go when danger comes to him, or when danger comes to someone else, or when danger comes to his own child, or when danger comes to a relative. Whether danger comes to him or to another, that is what he will do. He is not really strong. This is how it is. The truth is like this.

My love you. Do you understand?

A DISCIPLE

I have heard that before—not those words—but it just reaffirms what God has shown over and over, painfully, over and over again.

THE SHAIKH

A genuine father will be like that. He will not stay with everyone. It is very rare to live by his side. It is not an ordinary thing. If there is selfishness, the selfish love will be temporary and let go. A selfish attachment will let go, just as you let go. A selfish mother, father, guru, or shaikh may also be like that. They may also let go like that. If their profits start to decrease, they might let go.

These words are not only for the child who let go, they apply to all of you.

The fish that lives in the well knows the depth of the well. However, the insect that runs across the surface of the water will not know what lurks in the depths. The fish that lives in the large pond knows the extent of the pond and its secret.

There is a type of insect that runs across the water on four legs. It walks on the surface of the water, but it does not know the depths of the pond. It runs only across the top. It has something like shoes on its feet and uses them to run on the water. It walks on water without knowing its depth. If the fish that lives down below comes up, it catches the insect just like that! The insect does not know those things. Only the fish knows.

Like this, you too are running on the surface of the pond of maya. You know how to walk on the surface of the sea. As to what is below, you do not know its secret. You do not know those things. Only the fish that swims in the sea knows the seabed and the surface. Only an authentic and genuinely wise human being will have the wisdom to know the surface and the depth of life like this.

When you are running across the surface, you should not think, "We have discovered the secret that exists below. We know it." You are simply running across the surface. You should not run while your wisdom thinks, "We know the secrets below." That is dangerous. Like a fish, a Shaikh, a father of wisdom, knows the surface and the seabed of maya.

If a fish comes up as you run across the surface, "*Tak! Mch!*" it will instantly catch you. That is one of the dangers. It will lie half buried in mud, hiding within it, and then it will instantly catch you, *tak!* You will not even know what happened. Like this, only a father of wisdom will know the surface and the depth of life.

He knows.

Your actions and the wisdom you have learned are like the insect that runs across the surface of the life of maya. You will not really understand the secrets below, the accidents that are about to happen in your life, nor what is about to come. Only someone who knows this thoroughly will understand what can catch you. You must think of this. He will tell you of each danger in each place before it is about to occur. *Tak, tak*! He will instruct you in each place.

You cannot take your intellect and put it into his. It will not be appropriate. We must not do that, saying, "What *we* do is correct."

You must think. Your intelligence runs fast, but as soon as you see something in front of you, you will run backward. And when you see something behind you, you will run forward. If you look back and see something behind you, you will run forward. If something is in front of you, you will run backward. That is all you can do. In the end, you will be caught. You may run and run to hide somewhere, but it will catch you. It will catch you and then kill you. You do not know how to see what is in front of you and behind you before you begin. You do not understand the path before you start.

Only someone with experience will understand the state of seeing what is in front as well as what is behind—he knows the section that is in front of you and what is lurking behind you before you set out. That person of wisdom, that father of wisdom, knows.

Only if you stand in his section will he tell you, "This is what exists on this path. That is what exists on that path. Go this way! Then you can escape. Or else, just follow me." Then you can escape.

If you proceed, thinking, "I know," you will have to run from what is following you. You will run into darkness looking for a hiding place. When something comes at you from the front you will run backward and try to hide somewhere else. Yet you will simply be going towards another thing that is approaching you. Then you will be caught. Even though you may have great weapons such as guns, when danger comes, you will loudly scream, "*Haaaah!*" and drop those weapons. Those weapons cannot do anything for you. You will just drop them. That which was following you will catch you and finish you off.

This is the reason we need a father of wisdom. We need him for protection and for avoiding the accidents. We need a good man with good qualities—someone with love. Understand? Very well. Please think, all of you.

If you have wisdom, you must endeavor to think of what the consequences of your actions will be, whether they will be good or whether they will be bad. *Thank you.*

December 8, 1981
THE TREE OF TRUTH

Precious jeweled lights of my eyes, we have all gathered together. There is a reason why we—a father and his children—have gathered in one place.

There is a reason. There is a relationship.

If there is fruit in a tree, all kinds of birds will come to it from all kinds of places. The fruit is not there only for one kind of bird. They all like fruit. Is that fruit only for one species? No. Is it exclusively for the mynah, the parrot, or the dove? No. If there is fruit on that tree, all of God's creations who live on that fruit can come to that tree to search for it. All who love that fruit will come to search for that fruit, and each will take from it according to the capacity of its stomach.

That tree belongs in common to all of them. The fruits that ripen on it rightfully belong to everyone. There is nothing like class or race discrimination there.

Truth too is like that. The tree is truth. Everyone can take from it and cheerfully alleviate their hunger. They can be happy and delight in the fruit. Everyone will come to search for that tree. You and we have gathered here exactly like that to search for truth under the shade of a tree. That is why we meet here.

There is some kind of fruit here. There is some kind of taste here. There is a peace in it and tranquility. That is the reason each one of us searches for it with his own heart and goes to the place where the fruit is ripening. That is where we meet, where we gather. Truth is like the fruit on that tree. We are searching for the taste of truth, wisdom, *gnānam,* and God's love. We meet here to look for that taste—for truth.

When we gather like this, it will depend on which qualities we prefer to use when we taste the fruit. We will understand the taste according to our qualities. That is how we will be able to know its taste.

It will depend upon what kind of tongue you possess, what kind of thought you possess, what kind of wish you possess. There is no difference in the tree. The fruits are not different. The smell, the qualities, the fragrance, and the taste in the fruits are all the same. Many species, many colors, many complexions, many kinds of birds and fowl will come to it. They will experience the taste of the fruits depending upon their own actions and tongues. It is not the fault of the tree or the fruit. That is natural.

If they stay with the taste of that tree, they will know its taste. If they possess the taste when they taste the fruit, they will know the taste. It will have no differences. It is like this for the children who are searching for God, the children who love the taste of God, and who want to know God—that is how we will come to the tree.

However, if the actions of our own intellect were to fall on the fruit when we study wisdom, we would experience the taste of our own intellect. We would experience our own qualities. Our kinship attachments and desires would have the same effect. We would experience our own separations, our own differences of race, religion, and class. This is what we would see and experience. That is not what the fruit tastes like. If we want to know the taste of the fruit, we would have to dwell with the fruit, and then we would know. Then we would know the happiness.

Children, we too are like that. We have many qualities and many actions; we are of many races and religions and we have many desires and attachments. We are here with them. If we were to take those thoughts with us when we go to taste the grace of God, we would not taste grace, we would taste ourselves. We would taste our own qualities. We would taste the flavor of whatever we take with us. That is the difficulty.

Then we would have to find fault with it and the trouble would start. We have to think of this and stop doing that. It is only if we fall into the taste of the fruit that we can taste the real taste. We must taste it with the correct tongue. Only then can we know the taste. This is what we must think of, each child.

We must think of this, meet under the tree, and understand that the fruit we are tasting is the fruit of one tree, one group, one *family*.

This morning one of the disciples said something to me. She had been worrying about something for two or three days. She had read something about the Guru and then she began to worry.

What she had read described how very difficult it was to stay with a Shaikh, that it was very difficult to stay with a Shaikh. Is that correct?

A DISCIPLE

It was your discourse.

BAWA MUHAIYADDEEN ☮

It was in a discourse. This was what she was thinking: "How can I do this? It is very difficult to stay with the Shaikh. It is exactly as he described; it is very difficult for me. I have a husband. It is difficult to stay with the Shaikh, and now I have a husband. Should I do this, or should I do that? What kind of situation is this? I'm in the midst of a great difficulty." She was worrying like this in many ways. Knowing that, I called for her and she told me. "It is extremely difficult to stay with the Shaikh."

"That's certainly true," I said. "It is certainly difficult." But what else are you going to live with? Where can a child who has been with me go? What are you going to live with in peace?

The rain falls. Destruction can come from rain. There can be profit and there can be loss. There can be clouds. You may build a beautiful house and an earthquake can come. That is natural. The leaves will fall from the trees according to their limit. We too will abide by our limit. The ground gets cold. In the skies there can be thunder and lightning chasing the clouds. The sun, the darkness, and the day can be hidden by the clouds. They can conceal the moon and the stars.

From the time it is born, each thing in God's creation can make another disappear. The deer runs in fear for its life. Another creature is coming to catch and eat it. One creature catches while the other runs. Is that peace? All created things kill each other. They eat each other. They live in the rain, the heat of the sun, the wind, the clouds, and the earth, and they eat. The plants are the same when they grow. Then it is cold. They all grow. All created things such as the fish, the things in the sea, the things on the shore, all things are like this. None of them live in peace, do they? Are there any that live in tranquility? No. Do any of them lead serene lives? Nothing lives like that.

Is the water able to stay in one place? No, it flows. Does the water in the ocean stay in the ocean? It ebbs and flows, comes to the shore and goes back. Nothing that has come to the world, nothing that has appeared in all of creation, lives in peace, tranquility, or serenity.

Will mind and desire obtain peace in the ocean of maya? Will peace come to them there? Will the soul have peace there? Will desire ever find fulfillment and peace? Will you ever have enough clothing? Will you ever stop wanting new clothes to wear? Will you ever stop wanting food? Will sleep give you peace? It will not. Will peace come from staying awake? Will peace come from meditating?

There is mind and desire and the section of the body; there is the section of the soul; and there is the secret of God. There is the world of the earth that is hell; there is the world of the soul; and God's world. These are the three worlds. In which of these three worlds can you gain peace? Which place can bring you peace? Which one can bring you tranquility?

It is not like that. As long as we live our lives in the ocean of maya, we will never find peace. There is only one way to find peace. When the explanation comes to us to a certain extent, about what we have to see and what we have to discard in order to find peace, it will be like standing in front of a mirror and making ourselves *clear*. The work is to stay in front of the Shaikh, *clearing* ourselves.

You need a mirror if you want to make yourself beautiful. Before you go on a journey, you look at it. You comb your hair and so forth. You turn around and look back at it. You look at the mirror and when everything is adjusted properly and correctly, you leave. You check your clothing and everything. This is what you do before you go on a journey.

It is like this for your soul's journey too. You need a Shaikh for the journey of your soul. When you go there the work is to make yourself *clear* with wisdom. You must make your life *clear*, your mind *clear*, your ignorance *clear*, your qualities *clear*, your actions *clear*. You need a Shaikh to make yourself *clear* like this. When you come to the mirror, it will show you how to do the work of making yourself *clear*. It will show you.

It will show you yourself.

Then you can make yourself *clear*, you can make yourself beautiful. You must endeavor to live with a Shaikh just as you live with a mirror in a hallway of your house. He will show you each thing, one by one. If you have a mirror and if you look into it, you will see yourself, will you not?

If instead you think, "If I stay with the mirror, it will be difficult for me to live like that!" you will not see yourself or what your clothing looks like and then everything you do will be a mistake. You can certainly get dressed without looking into a mirror, but others may laugh at you. If you look at the mirror and make yourself *clear* first, it will be better.

It will be like throwing a mirror on the ground and saying, "This is a problem. It is a problem for my marriage!" To have a Shaikh is a problem. He will show you your actions and your conduct and everything that you have to *clear* away. He is there to show you so you can make yourself *clear*. He is there so you can make yourself beautiful. He will show you the clarity of beauty beyond beauty, good qualities beyond good qualities, good deeds beyond good deeds, patience beyond patience, peace beyond peace, tranquility beyond tranquility, wisdom beyond wisdom, truth beyond truth, *gnānam* beyond *gnānam*, grace beyond grace, resplendence beyond resplendence. It will elevate your path. It will elevate your life. It will elevate your nature. It will elevate your goodness.

A Shaikh is there to show you this. He is a mirror.

Thus, as each thing is made *clear*, there will be some distress. If you ask a dog to go bathe, is it going to bathe? It will bathe only after you train it and teach it to bathe. Untrained, it will growl and bark when it sees the water! If you pick it up and put it into water, it will growl and bark, "*Grr, val, val, val!*" If you catch the dog and lead it to water, it will bark, "*Val, val, val!*"

Like this, when you have the dog known as desire and the monkey known as the mind and you go to wash them, will they stand still after you catch them? No. They will scratch and bite as much as they can. This monkey and this dog will both act like this. We shouldn't let the dog run away or be afraid that it will bite. This is what a dog will do. Somehow we have to give the dog of desire a bath. We have to put a leash on it, pull it, and somehow get it into the water. Even if we can only pour water onto its head and body, we still have to scrub it and wash it. Will it stand still for this? It will leave.

Like this, children, you must do this with your thoughts and opinions, your desires and attachments, your religions and social classes, your scriptures and philosophies, the world and maya, the five elements, the colors and the complexions, the sexual games and amusements, the arts and the knowledge of the arts, food and drink, desire and mind. They will pursue you and control you.

We must *clear* them away. If you run away from the mirror, your beauty will immediately be destroyed. You will not be able to see yourself. It will be difficult to smile at it and difficult to run and live somewhere else. While you are making yourself *clear*, it will be difficult. But will you get peace if you run away? You will also have difficulty in another place. But there it will be more ugly, more difficult, and more crazy.

Therefore, you must stay and hold on. If you can stay, hold on, and make yourself *clear*, only exaltedness will come from it and peace beyond peace, tranquility beyond tranquility, justice beyond justice, compassion beyond compassion, unity beyond unity, patience beyond patience. Think of this.

If you become afraid of the mirror and run away, thinking, "Here I have to do everything over and over! It is too difficult to stay with the Shaikh. If I run away, I can escape," then that will be your fate.

Precious jeweled lights of my eyes, when the Shaikh is *clearing* away these things, he may hit you, he may criticize you, he may seem angry with you, he may scold you, he may shout at you, but you have to stay, withstand all of it, and hold on so you can see the path where you will find comfort. You must stay and hold on in that state.

My love you, children, jeweled lights of my eyes! This is the way for you to attain peace in that state. I am watching over you. The Shaikh is a mirror in your life. He will show you each one of your flaws with his wisdom, with his words, with his actions, and with his qualities. Then, like pouring water on a dog, he will wash away the ugly things in us.

Yet, if we pour water onto fire, it will hiss.

When its opposite is poured onto each thing, it will be difficult for that thing. In the midst of that difficulty, you have to think and use your wisdom: "This is what is actually creating the difficulty for me. When the opposite thing comes and creates a difficulty, the difficulty also comes to me. Yet, the opposite thing is not the problem. It is this original thing that is causing me difficulty." Then you must have the determination to say: "I too must join in to drive this thing away. This thing is difficult for me and it is difficult for others who are with me." If you can be like that and if you can establish that state, you can find exaltedness, peace, and tranquility in your life. Then the kingdom of God will be yours. Then the wealth of the kingdom of the soul, the kingdom of the world, and the kingdom of God will be yours. Then your life will be your life. You must somehow hold on to the Shaikh, jeweled lights of my eyes.

The skies, the sun, and the moon all live in suffering. They all suffer. One covers the other, and the other covers yet another and another. The clouds cover them. The darkness covers the moon. More darkness covers the stars. The water covers the mountains. The shadows cover them. Each one covers another like this. Each one makes the other suffer. Each thing attacks the other. That other attacks another and another and another. Who has peace? The weeds and the grasses?

A weed will choke out other plants. A cow will bite off the weed. Do they have peace? If you plant a beautiful crop, it will be cut down and harvested. Does a plant have peace? Does a flower have peace? Or is it fighting something? Like this, creation will never reach peace. Even if you think mind and desire can attain peace, they cannot.

If you want peace, you must stay in a place of peace. If you want something to be at peace, it must stay in a place of peace.

The shade is under the tree. He who stays in the shade finds peace. The shade is under the tree. He who stays in the shade will not feel the heat. If you stand in the shade of the Shaikh when waves from the heat of life—the weariness produced by maya; the heat of the connection to maya, the connection to the earth, and the connection to the elements; the wind; the storms; the rain; the maya; the *nafs ammārah*; the desires; the attachments; the blood ties and the bondage to those blood ties; the social classes and the colors—come to attack us, it will be like standing in the shade of a tree.

The shade of the Shaikh is unaffected by these things and will give you soul-peace. In that shade there is greater peace for the soul than there is in the heat of the world. That is why you need a Shaikh. If there is a tree, and if you stand under the tree instead of running away because you are afraid of the difficulties, the losses, the weariness, and the suffering, you will have peace and tranquility.

If when you see the Shaikh, you think, "We have seen the Shaikh. We have reached him. Now we can finish our business, and leave," you may obtain happiness for a moment and you may even obtain peace for a moment, yet maya will come a little while later. The *nafs* will come a little while after that. Then the mind will come, the monkey will come, and the dog will come. Each will come for a short time.

When you join a group of dogs, they will join together to bite you and bark at you, "*Bah, bah, bah, bah!*" When you join a group of demons, the demons will join together and howl ferociously, "*Bla, bla, bla, bla.*" When you join a group of monkeys, they will pick at you and tear at you with their teeth. Any group you join will do something to you. These things will follow you wherever you go.

Is that the Shaikh's fault? No. As long as you stay in the shade of the Shaikh, it will be good. If you deviate and go somewhere else, you will have to go to a place without goodness. You need to go where there are no evils, you need to go on the good path. The paths on which God dwells will be open. The paths on which Truth dwells will be open. You need to choose the right path.

If you leave to stay with the animals, you will suffer. If you run back and forth, back and forth, you will end up with animals, birds, and demons that will catch you and bite you. Then you will suffer. It is not the Shaikh's fault. This is the suffering that will come to you. You will be bitten as soon as you set foot on those paths. If you deviate from the path of God, mind and desire will come to you. You must stay by the side of the Shaikh to alleviate your suffering just as you take comfort in the shade of a tree.

How should this be done? Children, jeweled lights of my eyes! Very well. No matter how much danger there may be, no matter the situation, a baby monkey will cling tightly to its mother. When the baby cries, "*Eee! Eee!*" the mother will pick it up and the baby will hold on to her no matter how far she has to leap. When a peaceful moment comes, the monkey will put down her baby to sit, eat, and do other things. The mother eats and the baby eats. When danger comes and the baby runs to the mother, she instantly picks it up and leaps away. When danger comes and the baby cries, "*Eee!*" the mother picks it up and runs. She leaps away and runs and runs. She jumps from tree to tree to tree. No matter how far she has to leap, the baby will not let go of her.

You have seen how tightly a baby monkey clings to its mother, and how it will not let go even when she has to jump through huge trees. It will hold on to her chest and belly. As long it holds on like that, no danger will come to the little one unless danger comes to the mother. If it does not let go, the baby will not die as long as the mother is alive. This is what a monkey will do.

Similarly, if you cling to the *qalb* of the Shaikh, if you hold on to his heart, he will leap away when danger comes. If you hold on to him, danger will not come to you. It will all depend on how you hold on. If you let go, you will suffer.

There is a saying about monkeys: "If the baby fails to hold on and falls, the other monkeys will no longer accept it into their group." If a child fails to hold on and falls, none of the other monkeys will accept it. If it tries to approach them, they will reject it, hit it, bite it, and drive it away until it dies. They will no longer accept it into their group.

Similarly, if you let go of the Guru, you will never get close to God. You will not merge with Him. *Paradise* will not accept you.

If you let go, if you let go of the truth and fall, the group that is One Family in *Paradise*, will not accept you. They will not accept you there because you will have failed to hold on to the relationship.

You have let go. If a monkey lets go of its mother and falls, the other monkeys will no longer accept it. That baby will wander off and die alone.

Similarly, if you let go of your hold on the place that is called the Shaikh, if you fail to hold on, the kingdom of God will not accept you. God and the kingdom of God will not accept you if you fall away from a genuine Shaikh. That group, that One Family, will not accept you. Truth will not accept you. If you fail, that is what will happen.

When a baby monkey clings so tightly to its mother, how should you cling to the Shaikh? The danger comes to you only if you fail to hold on. If you hold on to his heart, he will leap away before the danger can come to you. He will save you from danger. The monkey shows us this state.

If you hold on to the heart of an Insān Kāmil, he will never let danger come to you. You will never lose that safety. Danger will come to you only if danger comes to him. And if danger should come to him, he will die protecting you. The mother may die but the child will survive. If you hold on that is what will happen. Even if a monkey is shot, the child will survive if it holds on to her belly.

If you cling to the heart of the Shaikh like a baby monkey holds on to its mother, that will be the grip of the faith, certitude, and determination that is *īmān*. That is the grip of *īmān*, the grip of faith. The other is simply the grip of a monkey.

If a monkey grip does not let go, how should your faith grip the Shaikh? If you hold on, the danger will not come to you.

There are monkeys like human beings, and human beings like monkeys. However, a genuine human being lives like God and possesses God's qualities, God's actions, God's justice, God's conscience, God's beauty, God's Light, and God's Resplendence. You must stay with that Beautiful Being and hold on to him without fail. Only then can you obtain the reward.

Look. The animals are all there: the birds, the fowl, the four-legged animals, and those that crawl on the ground. They all have babies and children. People too have babies and children. When danger comes to them, they leave their children and run away. Cattle, goats, and people give birth to children. When danger comes to attack them, they do not think of where their children are, they run away. The children of the cattle and goats run away with them. The parents run and the children have to follow them. A lion always catches the children first. The parents try to escape while the children are caught. Similarly, when suffering comes to people, they will try to escape like animals, without considering their young. A person will not be as careful or hold on as tightly as a monkey. Some animals are also like that. Birds are like that.

People too will run from danger and tell their children, "Follow me!" instead of protecting them. This is also what class distinctions, religions, doctrines, relatives, worldly ties, and blood ties will do. They will care only for their own safety. They will not stay there, because they would die too. They have to run to save themselves. They run.

However, the monkey will protect her child even if she has to die. A Shaikh is like that too, as long as you cling to him with the same kind of grip. The other animals will all run from danger and abandon their children, but if you hold on to God, if you hold on to the Truth, it will protect you. You must think of this. Each child must think of what it means to hold on to the Shaikh and understand how you must hold on to him. You must at least cling to him as tightly as a baby monkey clings to its mother. The disciple-children must hold on to the heart of their father with faith, without letting go.

It is certainly difficult. It is difficult to cling to the qualities, actions, behavior, love, goodness, compassion, patience, tolerance, and peace. It is difficult to establish that state of peace.

It is easy for a child to put sand in its hair. However, it is difficult for a mother to wash it away. It is a lot of work for the mother. It is easy for a child to play and put sand in its hair. It is easy for it to roll around and lie in the mud. It is difficult for the mother who has to *clear* it away. Who experiences the greater difficulty? The mother. Is it difficult for the child who puts the sand in its hair? Similarly, it is *easy, easy* for you to play. However, washing you, making you beautiful and *clear*, washing your clothes, and washing out the dirt in your hair is difficult. It is not difficult for you. There is no difficulty whatsoever for you.

You do not have the difficulty the Shaikh has. Look at how

difficult it is for a mother. The difficulty a Shaikh has in raising a child is a hundred times worse. You are always trying to get into the mud, the dirt, the *najis*, the unclean, the sin, and the hell somewhere. That is where you spend your time. The Shaikh has to wash you, cleanse you, bathe you, get the sand out of your hair, wash your hair, pick the nits out of it, and comb it, each time. It is very difficult. You just want to play in the mud and put sand in your hair. If you think about it, you will understand. Thus, the difficulty is his. It is not difficult for you.

Therefore, think about holding on to him with at least a monkey grip. All you have to do is hold on with your faith, determination, and certitude. That is the point you must reach at the correct place in order to attain the proper state so that you will be saved from danger.

If you do not, the sand you put in your hair will get into your eyes, and then you will cry. If you walk and play in the mud, you will slip and fall into it. You carry the consequences with you.

Similarly, it is difficult to stay with the Shaikh—you do have to give up everything and leave it behind. But if your grip is correct and you cling onto his heart, he will protect you from danger as he proceeds. The grip brings peace. This is what the disciple-children, the children of the Shaikh, the children rightfully born to the Shaikh, will do. That is how you can escape from danger.

Until you cling to him like that, the ghosts, demons, evil spirits, elemental forces, dogs, monkeys, maya, darkness, and *shaitān* will catch you. And when they catch you, they will drink your blood. However, if you cling to the Shaikh, he will leap away the moment these things approach. If your grip is true, if you are true children, you will be the children who are saved from danger, the children who have reached peace, tranquility, and serenity.

There are people like the animals who save only themselves when danger comes. There are shaikhs and *sayyids* like that too. There are people who save only themselves when danger comes. When a difficulty comes, they save themselves by running away. When trouble comes, they save themselves and run away.

April 28, 1982
THE JOB

We must be like detectives on the path to God in our worldly duties in this *dunyā*, this world, and also when we follow the Shaikh.

There was once a senior officer in the process of hiring a competent person as a detective. He led the applicants up to the sixth floor of the police station. In the end, only one applicant was able to correctly state that there had been one hundred twenty-eight steps and to make detailed observations about them. The others all merely followed the officer up the stairs.

Similarly, the Shaikh will be checking the lessons you learn while you follow him in the world up the steps of your wisdom with *unarvu, unarchi, putti, madi, nutparivu,* and *pahut arivu*— perception, awareness, intelligence, assessment, insightful wisdom, and discerning wisdom. He will be checking to see how you climb the mountain to reach the summit. If you want the job, he will say, "Very well. You seem to want it. Come, follow me."

The steps in your life are all made of earth, fire, water, air, and ether. You must climb up and transcend everything you see in your life. You must move past those things and proceed beyond them. You must climb up.

After you go to the Shaikh and explain that you want the job, he will say, "So then, come, follow me." You must observe each point on your path.

First, you must know the earth. What is the source of your body, your birth? What is that point on your path? What are the details? What is its state? What is there? What is it doing? You must correctly observe this explanation.

Second is the fire of hunger, the turn to the left. What exists there? You must understand this in your life.

Third is air, the turn to the right. What is your air doing? What are the vapors of the breath doing? In what state do they operate? Are they making you tired? Are they causing exhaustion? Is your breath being blocked? In this section, you must discover the point at which the air—this breath, this vapor—works. How do these breaths, these vapors, spiritual practices, magic, and tricks work? What kind of work do these faculties perform? How does this world work? We must carefully observe the clues. We must understand them point by point by point.

Fourth is the clouds, the delusions in your life, the things that can mesmerize your wisdom, the things that can mesmerize your sense of judgment. This is all water, creation, delusion. What do these delusions do to you? What are their points? How do they mesmerize you? How do they approach you? How does the mind delude us like this? How does desire delude us? How does it change our state? We must pay careful attention to this. We must extract the point.

Fifth is maya, the ether. We must turn to the right side. In what state does your *nasīb*, your destiny, your limit, exist? What is the effect of maya? How many forms does it take? What kind of beauty does it display? What kinds of sections does it display? This is what you must understand on that step.

Sixth, you must go straight up. You must climb straight up, still moving to the right, on the path that goes to the West. At the sixth level, you must distinguish and discern everything as you examine what is there. You must distinguish and discern what is right, what is wrong, what is good, and what is evil. That is what you must do in your life. "This is what I must avoid. That is what I must keep. That is good, this is bad." You must check each thing on the path. After you have checked for right and wrong, after the sixth level, you will come to stand on a plateau.

You will stand there and the Shaikh will question you. "Very well. You have arrived here. What do you need? Do you want this job? Is this what you came for? Very well. What did you see along the way? What wonders did you see? Now that you have come here, what wonders did you see? What did you see on the path?"

Then you must describe your life in detail. If you just say, "*Uh, bah, bah, bah, bah!*" you will not have the requisite answer. You must understand the points on the path. Only then can you win the position. You must understand.

"How could you get here and not see anything?" the Shaikh will ask.

"We saw nothing," they will say.

"How did you get here?" he will ask.

"We climbed steps," they will say.

"How many steps? How many turns? To which side did you turn each time?" he will ask.

"We didn't pay attention to how we got here, we were just following you," they will say.

"If that's how it was, what was the point?" the Shaikh will say.

The observant person will say, "I saw." He will state what he saw on each step. "I observed what was on the first step and what was on the next step. I observed the clues on the left and the clues on the right and what they looked like. Then again, I observed the clues on the left, again I observed how many steps and what clues were on the right." He will describe all the details. He will describe each of the *symbols* there.

"That was the last *symbol*," he will say as he describes how many turns there were for the one hundred twenty-eight steps. "There were six turns, but the beginning was straight and the end was straight."

"You are correct. You are the one who is competent. This is *pērarivu*, Divine Luminous Wisdom, the seventh step. I see that you have the ability to observe," the Shaikh will say. Then he will show him the Light of the Nūr. "You are the one who has the ability. The others are not capable. They still need to learn."

It is like this that you must observe each point as you follow the Shaikh. You must see exactly what is there by the way he walks as he goes forward. You must observe what is in his words. What is contained in his actions? What is there in the way he walks? What must I see? What must I do? Each point needs to be deconstructed as you proceed. Your work is to pay attention to what he looks at and to take the map of the *maygnānam*, the genuine wisdom, with you. As you follow him, you must be able to comprehend and understand what is happening, and make a map for yourself so you can describe it later when you are questioned about it, so you can demonstrate competence.

If you just smoke a cigarette and chat about something to someone else in the group who is following him, there will be no point. The state of following him is subtle, extremely detailed, and precise. You must be able to pick up each point on the path that he traverses, each clue that appears between birth, death, and Judgment.

Only then can you reach that state. Only that is a state of competence. Only then can you do God's service and God's duty and become Man-God in God's kingdom. Only then can you become a human being, His son, and do His duty.

That is the state in which you will have to act, doing service in God's kingdom, doing what is just and right. If you do not pay attention to that state, if you merely follow him, you will see no clues. Your wisdom will not be *clear*, your attention will not be *clear*.

You need to have *dānam, nidānam, avadānam,* and *gnānam*:

- *dānam* [sacrifice] You must sacrifice yourself on your path.
- *nidānam* [caution] You must be very careful on this dangerous path. There must not only be that, but after leaving this step there is more.
- *avadānam* [prudence] You must proceed in a balanced way. The wind will push you, mind will push you, desire will push you, blood ties will push you, money will push you, maya will push you. They will all shout at you. *Avadānam* means you must proceed with balance. It is a very narrow and sharp path. Sharper than a sword and straighter than wisdom. It is very difficult to walk upon. If your attention fails, you will miss the clues and fall.

- *gnānam* [wisdom] When you cross the line, this will be *gnānam*. It is called *gnānam* when you can do the job. Then you will do duty in that kingdom in this manner in order to fulfill the needs of the people, to fulfill the needs of their minds, to end their suffering, and make them peaceful.

If you want to demonstrate your competence for this job, you must pay attention to every detail as you follow the Shaikh.

Day and night, your attention must be on his breath and on his words as you take in the point. You must take each word into account. You must take in each point. You must go into each word and analyze it. You must go into every gaze to see what he is seeing. You must see how he walks and then you must walk as he walks. You must see what exists in each detail on the ground. Are there snakes? Are there scorpions? How is he walking?

If you do things in this way, you will get the job. Only after you take all those things into account will you be given that position. "This is it. You have the competence," he will say. That is how a detective will be.

This world is a map and you are the detective. You are surrounded by criminals: the mind, the languages, the five elements, attachments, bondages, religions, ethnic groups, colors, complexions, possessions, properties, titles, and honors. All of them are criminals! Everything that exists in the body is a criminal. Everything in the world, in the body, and in the mind is a criminal. How are you going to catch those criminals? How are you going to catch them and lock them up?

The criminals of the world, the criminals who have stolen God's property, are earth, fire, water, air, and ether, arrogance, karma, maya, *tārahan, singhan, sūran,* the six evils, lechery, malice, miserliness, sexual infatuation, fanaticism, envy, intoxicants, lust, theft, murder, falsehood, that which is known as the "I" and the "you," religious and ethnic separations, differences, possessions, and properties. They are the criminals who have slipped and fallen away from God's justice. They are the criminals who have slipped and fallen from His compassion. They are the criminals who have slipped and fallen from His love. They are the criminals who have slipped and fallen from His unity and are selfishly stealing things for themselves.

How are you going to catch these criminals?

How careful you must be at every moment if you want to catch and lock up these criminals! You must watch each step you take and understand what is there. If you do not take this kind of care you will never catch the criminals in this kingdom. The criminals will catch and kill you instead. The criminals will overcome and kill you. If you want to arrest these criminals and imprison them where they should be imprisoned, you must pay attention. It is not easy.

This point is most important if you want to catch and lock up these criminals and establish the justice of God and God's kingdom so there can be peace, tranquility, and serenity for all lives, if you want to establish God's state, if you want this job. That attention, those actions, and those qualities are most important for catching these criminals. You must pay attention. Then you can take the exam and get the job. You can prepare for it and learn from the Shaikh how to dedicate God's kingdom to God and make the people peaceful. You can catch all the criminals, lock them up, and punish them in the correct way.

Otherwise, if you say, "I am following the Shaikh, the Guru," and you proceed without any accountability, without understanding the situation, you will know nothing about your life when he asks you about it at the time you get there.

If you are not careful, the criminals will kill you. The elements will kill you. The maya will kill you. The evil qualities will kill you.

You must think like this about the state in which you need to live in order to obtain that position. This is the exalted state in which you must follow your Shaikh. You need to understand. Understand? If you understand, you must begin to learn.

How much work it is to get this position, how much care must be taken with each thing! *My love you*, my sons, my daughters, my grandchildren. Think about how you can reach this state and obtain this position.

May God help you. May He give you the strength, the wisdom, and the *īmān*. *Āmīn*.

May 17, 1982
THE FAITH

Disturbances of the mind, instabilities of the mind, contradictions of the mind, and tiredness in life come to every child. However, if the tiredness appears while you are in a place of truth, if the contradictions appear even after you have gone to God Himself, if the tiredness appears in a place of eternal justice, what is the reason?

Faith. It is because your faith is not strong. It is weak. It is because of a weakness in determined faith and certitude, a weakness of faith in God, faith in His Power. It is because of a weakness in faith that those circumstances arise.

Truth must have faith in truth. Justice must speak up for justice and have faith in it. God's qualities must have faith in God. That point must exist. If it takes root, if that *supreme root* establishes itself deep in truth, then the instability and tiredness will not arise.

Let's look at a tree. A tree has a *supreme root* that grows down with supporting roots surrounding it. The supporting roots can be pulled out at any time—during a storm, a difficulty, a strong wind, or a heavy rain. They can be pulled out, can they not? The *supreme root* protects them from the storms and strong winds. Because the *supreme root* is firm, it does not matter in which direction the tree sways. It does not matter what kind of strong wind, storm, or heavy rain comes. The tree is strong because of the *supreme root*. Its strength does not come from the supporting roots. The *supreme root* is its strength. That is what makes it strong.

Similarly, the supporting roots in man are the mind and the five elements that hold on to the surface. Faith in God, firm certitude, wisdom, determination, and good qualities must be strong and grow deep into truth. The storms that mind and desire bring—blood ties, religions, ethnic groups, colors, complexions, relatives, relationships, love, maya, darkness, hunger, illness, and old age—will attack.

Thus, when such storms attack him, he will not rely on the supporting roots for help if his life is held up by a *supreme root* like that of a tree which grows deep down with determined strength and holds up the tree. It will hold up his life, because that is a thing that does not break or fall. Thus it remains strong when the storms brought by mind, desire, maya, and darkness strike him. They will be naturally defeated.

However, if the tree does not have that strong root at that time and if it expects help from the supporting roots, the tree will fall. If it looks for help from its supporting roots, the tree will fall.

Similarly, man's supporting roots are earth, fire, water, air, and ether. If man expects this help, this support, and if the point that is the root of faith in God, certitude, and determination does not grow deep, expecting help from the elements will not be an intelligent decision. They are not stable things. They can change. They will change during suffering—that support departs during suffering.

All the deities, gods, idols, illusions, *shaktis*,[12] cells, and anything made of the five elements will change. As soon as suffering strikes, they will stop supporting you—they will run away. They will fly off! They will change. The five elements and intellect will change. Your perceptions will change. Your awareness will change. The instant suffering comes, they will not stay with you any longer. The instant difficulty comes, your perceptions will deteriorate. The instant more difficulty arrives, even your intellect will deteriorate. Scripture is limited by intellect. The limits of scripture are the limits of intellect. These supporting limits are the world. They are not strong and they will change during suffering. Your perceptions will deteriorate, your

---

12 *shaktis*   forces, energies

awareness will deteriorate, and your intellect will change. They are not strong. They cannot help us.

We need something strong. We need God's help because it is strong. We must believe in One God, that Power.

The other things are *shaktis* that can change. The *supreme root* is an immutable strength. If you can bring it into being and if it is strong, that *supreme root* is a strength that will never change. If you do not have this strength, the tiredness and the contradictions will come to you regularly, and the disturbances will come to your heart, changing section by section. You will never have peace if you do not have this strength when the storms come to attack you and when those things change.

Suffering comes to you because your *supreme root* is weak, because it has not grown deep. You have no peace because you have not driven out the suffering and the problems and the things that should be driven out. You have no peace in your life. You have no peace on the path to God. The root has not grown deep into that point on the path to God. Because the root has not grown deep, your life has not benefited. Then there could be disturbances. The cause of this is weakness.

When we look at a tree, we see that it obtains its own food after the *supreme root* has grown down into the ground. It obtains water and fertilizer and takes care of itself. The results are good—the fruit ripens, and the tree takes care of itself while being useful to others. It takes its own food from below and gives of itself in order to be useful to others. It has peace in its own life and it gives peace to others, does it not? The tree does both these things. It obtains peace for itself and gives peace to others.

It does not waver amid the storms, strong winds, thunder, and lightning that come. It does not waver, even though it is struck by all those things. It bends and yields, but it stands strong. It is made strong by the strength of the *supreme root*. That is its work. It takes care of itself and establishes its own state. It obtains its own food. The tree gets all those things from God because its *supreme root* has grown deep.

As soon as the fruit emerges, the tree gives that fruit to other beings. Similarly, when the *supreme root* known as firm faith in God grows deep in a human being, he will be able to obtain peace in his life. He will obtain nourishment wherever he is. He will have two sections just as a tree does. He will draw nourishment from God's section for the liberation of his soul, and then he will share the benefit that comes from it with the people. He will share the benefits. Thus, he will do two duties in two ways by sharing the benefits. Through doing so, he will obtain peace.

However, children, everyone who wears a body made of the five elements will have these difficulties. Why? Only God does not have this form. He does not have this form.

You are not alone, it is the same for me. In truth, I get tired sometimes, just as you do. Why? When you look out from that which is known as truth, certain difficulties do come. Some of the children are suffering, some of the children have pain, some of the children have difficulties, some of the children have illnesses, and when these things come to them, I say, "O God! Why do they have these difficulties? *Pāvam*, what a pity. Please protect them."

That is what causes me to suffer at that time. For a second, the suffering comes. But because my faith is strong, the suffering attacks me for only one or two seconds. It tries to shake me and then it leaves. Why? Because I have a body. I too have a body like you do. I have the section of the body like you do. Because God does not have it, it is easy for Him. The troubles come to us because we have bodies. The troubles will come and go. But we must be strong. We must have that faith and that certitude. Otherwise, there will be no peace in either section.

Just as a tree draws in its own nourishment for peace in its own life, we must give peace to others and have peace for ourselves by obtaining peace from doing God's duty and having good qualities. The tree gets peace for itself by giving peace to the lives of others.

Without that strength, you will not be able to obtain soul-peace like this, nor will you be able to obtain life-peace in the world. It is only through faith that you can search for wisdom, knowledge, and good qualities. If we search for this, we will have soul-peace and peace in our lives, and be able to perform God's duties. We must think of this, children. We must think of this.

For these hundred years, children, it will be possible to attain life-peace and soul-peace here. Only here has the way to peace been revealed. If you have certitude, you can get peace here. If you have wisdom, faith, certitude, and determination, this is the place for you to obtain these two kinds of peace. This is the chance that has come for these hundred years.

However, if you need miracles, if you are searching for miracles, you should realize that all living things, all six kinds of lives, have inherent abilities—from the ninety-six abilities of a human being to those that have only one level of wisdom.

All the poisonous beings perform miracles. They make others shake with fear. Some beings are crocodiles and some are lions. Tigers, poisonous snakes, and even ants perform miraculous feats that can make others tremble. Earth, fire, water, air, ether, maya, and darkness can all make others tremble. They have animal qualities, poisonous qualities.

Those qualities operate in all created things. Fire burns down a house. Water destroys the world. Air can break so many things. The earth can move—it can quake once and annihilate great, great cities. A thunderbolt, a lightning strike, can shake everything as it passes by. These are indeed miracles. They can do so much.

If a snake bites someone, he may go into convulsions and die. Similarly, when a tiger seizes him, it will grab him by his neck, drink his blood, and eat his liver. These are indeed miraculous acts. Attacking another is a miracle. Attacking another, putting on a display, and taking pride in yourself for doing so is a miracle. This is what animals do. To destroy another and to be proud of it is a miracle.

However, these things are not actually miracles.

My love you, my children. The miracle is finding peace within yourself. Finding peace in your own life is the miracle. To have peace on the wisdom side and to have peace in your life, to find peace on both sides of your life, is the miracle. This is something hardly anyone can do!

If you can do it, that will be the miracle in your life.

If you can do it, you can obtain soul-peace and life-peace. When everyone has peace and you can live without harming other lives, without killing any life, without causing suffering to any life, without destroying anything, you will have soul-peace and life-peace. Then all lives will live in a state of peace. You will reach peace within yourself and you will be able to show peace to the lives of others. To obtain that benefit is the miracle. That is the miracle you will see. That is the miracle for you. That is what hardly anyone can do!

To control the mind and to just be is the most exalted state.

Man can accomplish all else except this one thing. He can do everything else. Man cannot accomplish this one thing. If you accomplish this, it will be a miracle. If you can accomplish this, you will have peace in both sections—your soul will be at peace and your life will be at peace.

You must study wisdom in order to obtain wisdom and good qualities. You must study God's qualities and God's divine wisdom. You must search for both. There is no necessity for you to search for miracles. The miracles are within you. You must know that the miracle is to find peace within yourself.

This praise: "I am god, you are god, I am the greatest, you are the greatest," is not a miracle. The peace that man finds within himself is the miracle.

You alone will know. You will know the good and the evil. You will know the right and the wrong. No matter what you do, the warning will come to you afterward: "What you did was wrong. *Chee, chee, chee!* What you did was wrong. Why did you hit him? Why did you criticize him?" it will say. No matter what you do, the warning will come to you. It will come afterward, saying to you, "What you did was wrong. He is a good man."

Judgment is within you. The decision between right and wrong is within you. You yourself know the meaning of the good and the evil in what you have done. The warning comes. The judgment and the justice are there to show you and to make you aware of everything you have done. Wisdom makes it *clear* and reveals it to you.

You need no other court—the court is within you. You need no other judgment—the judgment is within you. You need no other hell or heaven or judgment—those places are within you. The warnings regarding good and evil are within you. They do not exist outside. Everything is within you. There is no separate truth. It is there within you so you can understand. The lessons are within you for your understanding. Your lessons are warning you, are they not?

You need a man of wisdom, God's qualities, and God's divine wisdom to make them function correctly. For this point, you must search for wisdom in order to obtain peace in both sections, to know what you need to know, and to be *clear* about this *clear* task.

In these hundred years, you need to find a man of wisdom—a man with good qualities, a man with God's qualities—and learn from him.

However, living as a five-element-being is difficult for everyone. Although he has given up his attachment to the world, although he has given up his connection to the world while living amid the five elements, the Shaikh will still be attached to his children on the path to God. Certain difficulties will arise because of those attachments. The children's difficulties will also come to him. When he is suffering from a child's pain, a child's distress, a child's hunger, a child's poverty, or a child's difficulty, the affliction will attack him as well, and could cause him to tremble. It is because he too possesses a body.

He has given up the entire world, but because he also has your section, that section will come to shake him once, and then leave. It is not easy.

If he had given up even that attachment, he would just be God.

Because he has the attachment to take God's children to the shore, he is just a human being. He is a man, *insān*, a human being, an Insān Kāmil, a perfected human being.

The one with that attachment is an Insān Kāmil. He is indeed a representative of God but he has that attachment. He has an attachment to taking the children to unite with truth, does he not? He has a connection to the problems and the difficulties that come to them on the way.

Until he hands over the responsibility, certain accidents and difficulties can occur. He has to pick you up, put you down, wake you up, give you milk, and guide you through the difficulties. Those difficulties come to him at that time and remain until he hands over the responsibility. Those difficulties come to him on that journey until the way is open to handing the responsibility to God. He gets tired at times.

You need strong faith while he is taking you to God. He does not possess the world, but he possesses the attachment to liberating your soul, the attachment to taking the children of God to God, and handing them over to Him. Difficulties will arise on the path upon which he guides you. If you look back and fall when the illnesses, the diseases, the worlds, the sorrows, the confusions caused by the five elements, and the problems caused by mind and desire come to attack you, it will be a little difficult for him to pick you up, carry you, and guide you to safety. Even without that, it is difficult for him to take you and guide you to safety. It is difficult to take the children to the One to whom the children belong.

Does he have that attachment? He has that attachment. The difficulties also come to him because of that. However, they only shake him for a second or two and then they leave. Then they leave. Very well.

However, child, everyone who has taken form in this world might experience instabilities, contradictions, and sorrows like this. Only God will not. Even though it is like this, you must understand how suffering is caused and how the suffering can come from each of your thoughts. Ethnicities, attachments, blood ties, religions, colors, complexions, cities, nations, homes, sexual obsessions, hatreds, and so forth—the weariness comes when the connection comes. The connection is the cause. It does not come through God. It is our own weakness.

If the *supreme root* takes hold, the branches of the tree will be good and strong, and you can hold on to them firmly and climb the tree. You can hold on to the good, strong branches of the tree and climb up to pick the fruit.

If we grab the branches of maya because they appear to be branches, we will fall. If we fall, there will be danger. There will be glittering fruits of maya, fruits that put on a good show. If we pick them, we will fall.

It was a show.

We did not use our wisdom and we did not have certitude. If we had certitude, we would not have picked the fruit, we would have understood. If we fall because of these things, we will experience danger and difficulty.

That which is called God has a greater strength. Everything that ripens there is the truth, the fruit of truth. That is the only fruit we should pick and eat. If we pick the other fruits, they will be maya, glitters, magic, and mesmerism. The moment we pick them, we will fall.

The moment you pick mantras, tricks, mesmerism, magic, drugs, LSD, marijuana, or opium, you will fall to the ground. It is ignorance. If you hold on to religions and prejudices—*tak!*—you will instantly fall and suffering will come from it. These calamities are our accidents. They are the problems that torment us.

If we reject them and hold on to that strong tree, it will bear the fruits of grace that are known as truth—beautiful fruits with varied tastes. Thus, we should pick them. They will be edible.

My children, *my love you*! You must think of this. You must establish your certitude and your strength. You must strengthen faith and certitude in God's name with firm determination. If you have that strength, strong winds and storms will come to you and shake you—but they will shake you and leave. They will work only for a short time. But if you are weak, they will subject you to much suffering and hardship. They will seize you and shake and shake and shake you for a long time.

My love you. There is a place in a motor from which the force originates. Some motors spin ten thousand times per minute, some spin fifteen thousand, some spin twenty thousand, some can spin even forty or fifty thousand times. The speed of the rotation determines the current that is generated.

Like this, the speed, the insight with which your wisdom spins, and how firmly your faith is pressed into certitude will determine how much current you generate for the section known as God. That will determine how much grace comes, how much Light comes, and how fast you can go.

When that state, that wisdom, and that ability exist in your heart, the faster it spins, the more the current will increase and increase and increase. The current is determined by the speed.

However, it must run with certitude; otherwise, it will explode. It will explode if it spins too fast; it will explode if it does not spin fast enough. A variation in the current, either less or more, will make it explode. It has a limit. It must spin according to its limits. The limit, the point, and the amount must be learned. The amount has to be calculated. At what time and in what manner should it spin? In what manner will it occur? If it goes in reverse, it will break; if it spins in the other direction, it will break.

Like this, if you want an Insān Kāmil to be of benefit to you, you must realize that God is a Power, a Motor that can light up the entire world and dispel the darkness.

God has put each power station in place—each station is an Insān Kāmil. The Light is supplied through them. The current is drawn through them. They are God's representatives, His power stations. God has placed them there, section by section, and when you go to those stations, each station will provide the supply for each section. That is what they will do. They are supply stations.

God is special. He is the Light, the Motor, the Sun that dispels the darkness. These stations exist to dispel the darkness of the mind and of life. That is why grace, wisdom, and God's qualities must be revealed through those who are Insān Kāmil. An Insān Kāmil will be like that. He will receive the current from the Motor and supply it to others. He must give it to you to dispel the darkness and to bring peace to your life. He is the one who can transmit the current. This is what a human being who is an Insān Kāmil will do.

He will become a human being and then he will become the Human Being known as Wisdom.

He will receive the wisdom, the qualities, and the truth and make them public. He will receive the point of truth and supply the wisdom to dispel the darkness and the delusions of life, and the suffering that comes from them. This is what an *insān* will do.

When an Insān Kāmil receives these things like that and supplies them to you, the public, he will have no attachment, no world, nothing. However, on the path upon which he has to take God's children and give them back to God, he will tremble if a difficulty comes to you. The suffering that comes to you also comes to him. Because of this, it will shake him for a moment. It will make him suffer a little, but then it will go. Before he can protect you, he will tremble. It will shake him, but then go.

Why? The attachment to giving God's children back to God has come to him. He has to open the way and guide you. He has that suffering. That is why this difficulty has arisen for him.

However, there is nothing to request of God. God knows everything, does He not? There is nothing He does not know. Without Him, not an atom would move. There is no place in which He does not exist. All souls are connected to Him. All truth is connected to Him. All good is connected to Him. It is all connected to Him. Those connections must pass through Him because there is nothing He does not know. There is nothing He does not understand, is there?

He is the One who gives food to the toad that lives hidden under the stone, to all the lives in the wombs [awaiting their birth], to the weeds, and to the grasses.[13] What can we possibly request of Him? There is no flaw about which to question Him. There is no room. He knows. Thus, there is no room to request anything.

If we were to ask for something, what could we request? When we correct our own faults, we will know what our suffering came from. It is not God's fault. We have to ask our own hearts, "What did this illness, this mistake, this suffering, come from?" We must ask our own hearts and end our own suffering. We must drive it out from there. The medicine for it is right there. We must ask ourselves, "This is connected to us, so what did it come from?"

The suffering came from within us. Each connection came from within us. Thus, that is what must be fixed. What can we request? He did not cause the suffering. There is nothing to ask Him. God does not attack anyone. There is creation, protection, and sustenance. He creates, protects, and sustains.

Yet if you are unable to rid yourself of suffering that you cannot bear, if you are unable to drive it out, you must surrender.

"There is nothing I can do now through my actions. O God, You do it!" You can say that only if the situation goes beyond your wisdom. If there is something that cannot be fixed with your own wisdom and God's qualities, then say those words. Then you can say: "I cannot do this, O God. I cannot fix this with my wisdom and my qualities. You must do this, and correct my mistake."

All the suffering that came to us before that moment came

---

13 This is a reference to the "Song of Moses ☉" a version of which can be found in *The Map of the Journey to God*. Bawa Muhaiyaddeen. Philadelphia: Fellowship Press, 2006. Print.

through us. Only we ourselves can fix what we ourselves have done. Only we can make the correction and *clear* it up. We created the illness.

It is your work to go to the bathroom by yourself and to wash yourself afterwards, is it not? You must clean the mat you sleep on before you lie down. You have to sweep the floor before you lie down. If you just lie down without doing that, the insects and the worms that live there will bite you and it will be your fault.

God has given you two eyes, two ears, two nostrils, a mouth, and two openings below. Should you not then understand? Understand and correct your own faults. Know what is right and wrong. What you have to do is your duty, your obligation. The state in which you have to accomplish it belongs to you and what you have to understand belongs to you. You have to fix things instead of asking God about them.

What is there to ask God about? Is it God's test? No. Does God need to punish you? No. Is God angry? No.

It is your mistake. When you correct your own mistakes, everything will be *cleared* up. Thus, there is nothing we need to request. We have no need to say, "God forgive us." If I correct the mistake I made, that is forgiveness. That is forgiveness. Thus, there is nothing we need to ask God. Any suffering, any difficulty that comes to us, comes through ourselves. That is the reason wisdom and God's qualities must become *clear*.

Search for that faith.

If we say, "O God protect me! Do this, do that!" that is already His duty, is it not? Creation, protection, and sustenance—He will do it. Do your duty. Then you will be at peace. If we know this, our lives will be heaven, the kingdom of heaven. There will be no kingdom of hell.

We are God's children. Our soul's liberation and our life will be a life of the kingdom of heaven. We will have freedom, peace, tranquility, unity, and solidarity. This is what we must understand. This is wisdom, the strength of wisdom. God's qualities and the truth are like that.

This is the reason you need an Insān Kāmil, a man, to publicly distribute and supply you with what comes from the Motor. He is the Human Being within the human being. He is the *Insān* within the human being. He is the Kāmil within the *insān*. He is the *Truth-Man*. You need him. You need his wisdom, qualities, actions, and duties. You must obtain the clarity from him in these hundred years. This place will be a somewhat good for these hundred years. You will be able to get a little clarity during that time.

You need faith.

You must have faith no matter what you look for. Any work you want to do must be done with faith, determination, and certitude. You must study wisdom and good qualities from someone who has that wisdom and those good qualities. You must get them from him and act accordingly.

If peace is to come to you, get it from someone who lives in peace. Get tranquility from someone who has tranquility. Get patience from someone who is patient. Get justice from someone who is just. When you get it, peace will exist in your life on both sides: soul-peace and life-peace, both sides. Then you will have peace in this world and peace in that world.

This is the miracle you must see. This is the miracle you must attain—peace. You will never see peace or get peace from any other miracle. What you see in yourself is peace. This is what you must search for. *My love you. Anbu.* Understand this.

Āmīn. May God help us.

Glossary

The following traditional supplications in Arabic are used throughout the text:

☺ *radiyAllāhu 'anhu* or *anhā*, may Allāh be pleased with him or her, is used following the name of a companion of the Prophet Muhammad ☺, *aqtāb*, wives of the prophets, and exalted saints.

☺ *'alaihis-salām*, peace be upon him, is used following the name of a prophet or an angel.

☺ *sallAllāhu 'alaihi wa sallam*, may Allāh bless him and grant him peace, is used after mentioning the name of Prophet Muhammad, the Rasūlullāh, the Messenger of Allāh.

Unless otherwise noted, the glossary words are Tamil, a Dravidian language whose origins in antiquity are unknown. Although the glossary has been assembled by editors and translators over the years, a majority of the explanations and definitions have come directly from Bawa Muhaiyaddeen ☺.

Pronunciation Key

The non-Arabic and non-Tamil reader of this book will encounter unknown words and names. We have tried to make them as simple as possible to pronounce.

While there are standard ways of transliterating Arabic letters into Roman script, there is no standard system of transliterating Tamil. Thus, we have not adopted any system in its entirety, but are indebted to many.

We have simplified the consonants—for the typical English speaking person, it would not be particularly helpful to distinguish between the two types of s or h or t in Arabic or the two types of t or the three types of n or l in Tamil.

> dh in Arabic is pronounced like the th in then
> kh in Arabic is pronoucded like the ch in the Scottish loch
> gn is pronounced like the ng in king or like the ñ in the Spanish word *mañana*
> k has been variously transliterated as k or h or g, because its sound is dependent upon its position in the Tamil word
> th (a confusing and inconsistently applied legacy Tamil transliteration that has come down to us from the German) has been simplified throughout as t or d, depending on its position, and thus sound, in the Tamil word

Both Arabic and Tamil have long and short vowels: the long vowels have been indicated by long marks in most cases. Thus, in Arabic and Tamil (except where noted):

> a   as in agree for Tamil;
>   as in either agree or apple for Arabic, depending on placement
> ā   as in father for Tamil;
>   as above with a lengthening of sound for Arabic
> i   as in pin
> ī   as in pique
> u   as in pull
> ū   as in rule

o	as in sock
ō	as in ore
e	as in end
ē	as in they
ai	as in aisle except at the end of a word, where it is generally pronounced as in day, for Tamil. In Arabic this may sound either like aisle or day, depending on the letter preceding it.

Any good transliteration system, of course, needs to be logically consistent. However, the idiosyncrasies of both languages must be considered; a few well-placed exceptions serve to clarify a sound that would otherwise be mangled. For instance, *nāi* (dog—pronounced as in high) could not be spelled *nāy* without causing confusion, even though that is what the Tamil spelling would seem to indicate.

A

'abd (Arabic n.) slave, servant
adhāb (Arabic n.) the punishment and torture in hell
agnānam lack of (n.) *gnānam*, wisdom
aiyō (interjection) an exclamation of surprise or sorrow
ākhirah (Arabic n.) The kingdom of God; *ākhirah* is where the soul proclaims the First Kalimah to Allāh. "There is nothing but You, O Allāh!" This is the ultimate and final realization, it is the soul's exclamation as it perceives who it is, and with this final realization and expression, the soul that is a ray of God's Light returns to the One Omnipresent God. The soul returns to the Source from which it came. There is only One— Allāh. Where all this happens is called *ākhirah*.
al-hamdu lillāh (Arabic phrase) all praise is to Allāh
āmīn (Arabic n.) may it be so
anbu (n.) love
an-bū (phrase) the flower of love. This is a combination word: *anbu* means love, *bū* means flower.
appā (n.) father

as-salāmu 'alaikum wa rahmatullāhi wa barakātahu (Arabic phrase) The peace and compassionate grace (and blessings) of God be upon you.

a'ūdhu billāhi minash-shaitānir-rajīm (Arabic phrase) I seek refuge in Allāh from the accursed satan.

avadānam (n.) prudence

awwal (Arabic. n.) the beginning, creation

B

Bismillāhir-Rahmānir-Rahīm (Arabic phrase) In the name of God, the Most Compassionate, the Most Merciful.

D

dānam (n.) sacrifice

dhikr (Arabic n.) The remembrance of God; of the many *dhikrs*, the most exalted *dhikr* is "*Lā ilāha illAllāhu*: There is nothing other than You, O God. Only You are Allāh." All *dhikrs* relate to His *wilāyāt* or His actions, but this *dhikr* points to Him and to Him alone.

dūlah (Arabic n.) wealth

dunyā (Arabic n.) world

E

en-sān (n.) eight-span

F

firdaus (Arabic n.) paradise

G

gnānam (n.) knowledge, knowledge of the divine

H

hadīth (Arabic n.) a tradition of the Prophet Muhammad ﷺ

hayāh (Arabic n.) life; lifetime

houris (Arabic n.) the duties you do here in this world that become the children who serve you in paradise

huwah (Arabic n.) the chasm [of fire]

I

ibādah (Arabic n.) service to God performed with a melting heart
'ilm (Arabic n.) knowledge of the divine
īmān (Arabic n.) absolute and unshakable faith that God alone exists; the complete acceptance by the heart that God is One
insān (Arabic n.) man, human being
Insān Kāmil (Arabic n.) a perfected human being; one who has realized Allāh as his only wealth, cutting away the wealth of the world and the wealth sought by the mind; one who has acquired God's qualities, performs his own actions accordingly, and immerses himself within those qualities; one in whom everything other than Allāh has been extinguished

J

jahannam (Arabic n.) the lowest hell
jinn (Arabic n.) a being created of fire

K

Ka'bah (Arabic n.) God's House of prayer in Mecca that Muslims face in their five daily prayers
khidmah (Arabic n.) service and duty

M

madi (n.) the fourth level of wisdom; assessment
malā'ikah (Arabic n.) angels, archangels
maut (Arabic n.) death
maya (n.) The glitters seen in the darkness of illusion; the 105 million glitters seen in the darkness of the mind which result in 105 million rebirths. Maya is a *shakti,* an energy, that can take many, many millions of hypnotic forms. If man tries to grasp these forms with his intellect, though he sees the form, he will never be able to catch it, for it will elude him by taking another form. Maya is a *shakti* which takes on various shapes, causes man to forfeit his wisdom, and confuses and hypnotizes him into a state of torpor. This word has many meanings. Lit. illusion
maygnānam (n.) true wisdom

mubārakāt (Tamil & Arabic n.) The blessings of God's love in all three worlds, the *awwal*, the *dunyā*, and the *ākhirah*. Allāh's wealth is the wealth of the soul, of wisdom, and of His grace, which is the resplendent wisdom of the Nūr. *Mu* (n.) is a Tamil prefix meaning three; *barakāt* (Arabic n.) means blessings.

mu'min (pl. *mu'minūn*) (Arabic n.) true believer(s)

N

nafs ammārahh (Arabic n.) the seven desires which goad and incite one towards evil

nasīb (Arabic n.) destiny
nidānam (n.) caution
nutparivu (n.) subtle wisdom; insightful wisdom

P

pahut arivu (n.) the sixth level of wisdom; discerning wisdom
pāvam (n.) What a pity.
pērarivu (n) the seventh level of wisdom; Divine Luminous Wisdom
purānas (n.) ancient histories
putti (n.) the third level of wisdom; intellect

Q

qabr (Arabic n.) the grave
qalb (Arabic n.) the heart, the heart within the heart of man, the innermost heart. Bawa Muhaiyaddeen☺ explains that there are two states for the *qalb*. One state is made up of four chambers, which represent Hinduism, Fire-Worship, Christianity, and Islām. Inside these four chambers there is a flower, the flower of the *qalb* that is the divine qualities of Allāh. This is the second state, the flower of grace, *rahmah*. God's fragrance exists within this inner *qalb*.
qalb-bu (n.) innermost heart-flower
qudrah (Arabic n.) the power of God

R

rahmah (Arabic n.) compassion, grace, mercy

Rahmatul-'ālamīn (Arabic phrase) the Mercy for All the Universes, the One who gives everything to all His creations

rūhānī (Arabic n.) elemental spirit

S

sabūr (Arabic n.) Patience; inner patience; to go within patience, to accept it, to think and reflect within it. *Sabūr* is that patience deep within patience which comforts, soothes, and alleviates the suffering caused by the mind. *Sabūr* is the intensive form of *sabr*

shaikh (Arabic n.) teacher

shaitān (Arabic n.) satan

shakti (n.) the energy or force of creation arising from the five elements

shukūr (Arabic n.) intense gratitude; contentment with whatever may happen, realizing that everything comes from Allāh; contentment arising from gratitude

T

tārahan, singhan, sūran (phrase) the three sons of maya, illusion

tawakkul (Arabic n.) trust (in Allāh)

tawakkul-'alAllāh (Arabic phrase) absolute trust in God; surrender to God; handing over to God the entire responsibility for everything

toluhay (n.) prayer, specifically the five-times prayer

U

unarchi (n.) the second level of wisdom; awareness

unarvu (n.) the first level of wisdom; perception

V

vāsi kudiray (phrase) the horse of the breath in the *dhikr*, *lā ilāha illAllāhu*, there is nothing other than You, O God. You are Allāh.

vēdas, vēdantas (n.) scriptures, doctrines

W

wilāyah (pl. *wilāyāt*) (Arabic n.) the miraculous duties and actions of Allāh.

Passim denotes that the references are not to be found on all of the listed pages, e.g., 24-29 *passim* would be used where the reference is on pages 24, 25, 27, and 29.

INDEX

A

air. *See* elements
al-hamdu lillāh (all praise is to God), 64
animals
    city and human, 5–6
    of the jungle, 4–6
    protect their children, 88–90
Ant-Man, 72
armadillo and elephant, 43–44
arrogance of the "I", 53, 55, 63
attachments Shaikh has to his children, 103–104
austerity and meditation, 4-5

B

bags of cotton, 13–15
barber and his sharp knife, 40–41
Bawa Muhaiyaddeen's ☮ lessons, 3–8
beetles, children of the Shaikh as, 12–14, 17
believers, 60
benefit, obtain the, 23
blood flows when we weep inside, 47, 49
body
    difficulties of having a, 100, 104
    eight-span, 6–7
boil, doctor lances the, 46
book within, 66, 68
branches of truth or maya, 104-105
breasts, father has two, 51–53. *See also* nipples

C

car, horn of a, 56–57

certitude, 41, 46-47, 72, 105. *See also* faith
chicks protected by hen, 74–75
child puts sand in hair causing difficulty, 89–90
children, Shaikh has few, 68–72
church, people look around in the, 18
clear yourself, 82–84
cling to the Shaikh, 87–90
clouds of doubt, 3
clues on the path. *See* path, clues on the
comfort and discomfort of the human being, 10–14
comparisons, make no, 52–56 *passim*
compassion of God, 55
competence on the path. *See* path, competence on the
connection to God, 49
control lives within, 36
correct your own faults, 108
cotton, bags of, 13–15
creatures eat one another, 82
criminal, everything is a, 95–96
crop, grow your, 20
current, 105-106
    Shaikh checks the—of the disciple, 30

D

dānam, nidānam, avadānam, and *gnānam* (sacrifice, caution, prudence, and wisdom), 94–95
danger that comes, 75, 87–90
darkness joined by clouds, 3
desert, 9–14 *passim*
desire, mind and, 84
detective(s) on the path to God, 91, 95
difficulty(ies) of staying with the Shaikh, 81-90 *passim*
    will come, 71–72, 100, 103–108
    See also suffering

disciples of the Shaikh, 29–38
diseases, operate on inner, 25–26. *See also* illnesses; sickness
doctor lances boil, 46
dog
    bathe a, 83–84
    licks, 21–22
doubt(s), 3, 48
dream
    of the mind, 26–27
    world is a, 12–14

E

eagle strikes, 74–75
earth. *See* elements
elements, five, 36, 91–92, 98, 101
elephant and armadillo, 43–44
enemies within, 35–36
ether, 4. *See also* elements
excrement, sugar to a dog, 22
explanations, inside and outside, 34–36
eyes, inner and outer, 47, 49

F

faith
    and certitude, 40–41
    grip of, 88–90
    leak in your, 40–41
    strength of, 15-16
    weakness in, 97. *See also* īmān
F(f)ather
    cuts sickness, 47
    has two breasts, 51–53
    purity of the kingdom of our, 8
    of wisdom, 2-3, 74–78
fault(s)
    of the child, 51–56 *passim*
    correct your own, 108
fire
    of hell, 7
    of sin, 41–48 *passim*
    of wisdom, 13–15
    See also elements

fish
    knows the depth of the water, 76
    movement of the—on the hook, 54
flower
    fragrance of the, 24, 58
    garden, 59–60
fool, Shaikh calls you a, 16
forgiveness, 108
fruit
    orchard, 59–60
    tastes of the, 80–81
    that belongs to everyone, 79–81
    tree, 53–54
    of truth, 105

G

gemstone, cutting a, 45–46
Gnāna Shaikh blocks all paths, 65–72
gnānam
    heaven of, 8
    study, 26
God
    compassion of, 55
    connection to, 49
    faith in, 98–100, 104–105, 109
    house of, 62, 64
    is a Motor, 106, 109
    knows everything, 107
    Light of, 45
    path to, 86–87, 91–94
    separation from, 55
    Shaikh gives child to, 37
    wealth of, 62–64
Guru
    Nādan, 42–49
    True—does not kill, 42–49
    you and the — are not two, 48
guru, ordinary, 65

H

hand
    of love, 73
    Shaikh takes your, 17

heart, 21
    all is within the, 59–60
    embraces others, 54–55, 60
    locked, 56
    open your, 55–64 *passim*. See also *qalb*
heaven of *gnānam*, 8
hell, 7, 42, 55
    house of, 61
    pillar in, 65
hen protects her chicks, 74–75
history within, 66–69
horn of a car, 56–57
houris, 59
house,
    of the body, 6–7
    build the—within the heart, 59–60
    of heaven, 62
    of hell, 61
    locked, 56
human
    animals, 5-6, 10
    being, 6–7, 10, 106, 109
        become a, 7–8
        comfort and discomfort of, 10–14
    hundred years, one chance for peace, 100-103 *passim*, 109
hunger, worldly and soul, 51–53
hunter wasp, Shaikh will prick each child like a, 31–38 *passim*

I

"I", arrogance of the, 53, 55, 63
ignorance, 73–74
illnesses, 67–68, 71
    heal your, 26. See also diseases; sickness
īmān is needed, 71–72. See also faith
inchworms, 31–34
insān (human being), 6–7
Insān Kāmil (perfected human being), 64, 109

Insān Kāmil (*continued*)
    difficulties of, 69-71
    each—is a power station for God, 106
    has attachment to his children, 103–104
    pain of staying with an, 45-46
    stay with an—for twelve years, 26
insect(s)
    dwelling under a tree, 10–13 *passim*
    that runs across the surface, 76–77
intellect, limits of, 98–99

J

journey of life, 9–13 *passim*
Judgment is within, 102
jungle
    animals of the, 4–5
    difficulties in a, 10

K

knife
    of the barber (the Shaikh), 40–41
    of wisdom, 24–25

L

leak in pond, 39–40
lessons, learn through purity, 7–8
life
    journey of, 9–13 *passim*
    -peace, 100-101, 109
    tiredness in, 97–100 *passim*
Light of God, 45
lives, control inner, 36
love
    hand of, 73
    your brothers and sisters, 54

M

man
    explanations given within, 34–36

man (*continued*)
    is the worst animal, 35–36
    storms attack, 97-99
man of wisdom
    children of a, 2
    find a, 103–106 *passim*, 109
    names for a, 2
    purity of a, 7-8
    searching for a, 1
marketplace, 69–70
meditation and austerity, 4-5
milk given from breast of the father, 51–53
mind
    and desire, 84
    dreams of the, 22, 26–27
    thoughts of the, 4
miracle(s)
    of animals, 101
    of finding peace within oneself, 101–102
mirage, 12, 14
mirror, Shaikh is a, 82–84
mistakes caused by doubt, 57
monkey baby clings to its mother, 87–89
moon dispels darkness, 3
mosque, people look around in the, 18
mouth of the disciple, 52-53, 56-57

N

nipple(s) of the father, 52–57 *passim*, 64
Nūr, Light of the, 93

O

opposite creates a difficulty, 85

P

pain comes to disciple, 41–49 *passim*
paradise, 62, 87

path(s)
    blocked, 65–72
    competence on the, 91-95 *passim*
    to God, 86–87, 91–94
    questions on the, 92-94
peace
    none live in, 82, 99
    one hundred years, chance for, 100-103 *passim*, 109
    of a tree, 99–100
    two kinds of, 99–103, 109
    will come, 11
person, wise, Shaikh calls you a, 16
pills, discourses are, 40
points
    on the path, 92–96
    taken in to the heart, 21-25 *passim*
pond, leak in, 39–40
pray, learn to, 67
purity of a man of wisdom, 7-8

Q

qalb must have strength, 15–16. See *also* heart
qalb-bū (flower of the heart), 58
qualities, good, learn, 26–27
    and actions of the animals, study, 5-6

R

rahmah, rain of grace, 20
rat in the rafters, distracted by, 19–20
reason we gather, 1
rivers within the heart, 59–60
root(s)
    supreme, 97–99, 104

S

self-business, 69–70

shade
- of the Shaikh, 86
- of a tree, 10–13, 17, 85–87

Shaikh
- as a barber, 40-41
- blocks all the paths, 65-72
- calls you a wise person or a fool, 16
- cling to the, 87–90
- difficult to stay with the, 81–90 *passim*
- disciples of the, 29-38
- follow the, 91–96
- get wisdom from the—while alive, 22-27
- gives the pills of discourses, 40
- has attachment to his children, 103–104
- has few children, 68–72
- has the fire of wisdom, 13–15
- intermingle with the, 26–27
- is a mirror, 82-84
- knife of the, 24-25, 40-41
- people do not listen to the, 18–22
- pricks his children, 31–33, 37–38
- *qalb* of the, 87
- search for the, 9–18 *passim*
- shade of the, 12–13, 86
- stay with the—for twelve years, 23–26 *passim*
- touch of the, 17
- what the—gives is very heavy, 15-16

sickness, Father cuts, 47. See also diseases; illnesses
soul-peace, 100-101, 109
sounds within, 35–36
spans, eight—of the body, 6–7
springs of grace, 62–64
statements, two—of the Shaikh, 16
station, power, each Insān Kamil is a, 106
stick of wisdom, 74
storms attack man, 97-99
strength of faith, 15–16
suffering comes, 85–87, 98–100, 106–108. See also difficulty(ies)

T

taste of truth, 80
temple, people look around in the, 18
thoughts, 4
- of the children in Sri Lanka, 21–23
- of the mind, 4

tiredness in life, 97-100 *passim*
touch of the Shaikh, 17
treasury, man is placed in the, 46
tree
- fruit, 53–54, 79–81
- peace of a, 99–100
- shade of a, 10–13, 17, 85–87
- supreme root of a, 97–100, 104

truth
- as a tree, 79–80
- hand of, 41
- is very heavy, 15–16
- value of, 15–17

Truth-Man, 44–46

W

warning comes within, 102
wasp, hunter, 31-38 *passim*
water
- drop of, 62–63
- in pond, 39–40
- -writing, 66
- *See also* elements

wealth of God, 62–64
weapon of wisdom, 24-25

wisdom
> dispels ignorance, 3
> father of, 3, 74–78
> fire of, 13–15
> knife of, 24–25
> known as heat, 66–67
> man of. *See* man of wisdom
> stick of, 74

worlds within, 34–36

Y

years, a hundred, chance for peace,
    100-103, *passim*, 109

M. R. Bawa Muhaiyaddeen ☙

The words of Muhammad Raheem Bawa Muhaiyaddeen ☙ reveal the Sufi path of esoteric Islām: that the human being is uniquely created with the faculty of wisdom, enabling him to trace himself back to his Origin—Allāh, the Creator and Cherisher of all the Universes who exists in unity with all lives—and to surrender to that Source, leaving the One, the Truth, as the only reality in his life. This is the original intention of the purity that is Islām.

Bawa Muhaiyaddeen ☙ spoke endlessly of this Truth through parables, discourses, songs, and stories, all pointing the way to return to God. Over fifteen thousand hours of this ocean of knowledge were recorded.

People of all ages, religions, classes, backgrounds, and races flocked to hear and be near him; he interacted compassionately and lovingly with all of them, opening his heart to them equally, regardless of who they were. Presidents of countries and fakirs from the streets, the proud and the humble, the high-ranking and the low-ranking, the ordinary and the extraordinary, the extremely poor and the extremely rich all sat side by side in his presence.

An extraordinary being, Bawa Muhaiyaddeen ☉ taught from experience, having traversed the path and returned, divinely aware — sent back to exhort all who yearn for the experience of God to discover the inner wisdom that is the path of surrender to that One.

Bawa Muhaiyaddeen ☉ did not tell us much about his life, although there were rare moments when he spoke to those gathered around him of certain memories.

What we know is that he was first sighted by spiritual seekers — a man we know only as Periari and a few others from the town of Kokuvil — at the edge of the jungle near the pilgrimage town of Kataragama in what was then known as the island country of Ceylon.

The tiny island that is shaped like a teardrop falling from the tip of southern India is a place known for its legendary as well as its sacred geography. Adam's Peak in the center of the island is said to have retained the imprint created by the impact of Adam's foot from when he first touched the earth after being cast out of the Garden of Eden.

Referred to in the ancient text of the *Ramayana* as Lanka, it was the site of Princess Sita's captivity by her abductor, Ravana, the evil demon-king of Lanka. The *Ramayana* contains details of the battlefields where the armies of her husband Prince Rama fought the armies of the demon-king, and describes the groves of exotic herbs dropped by Hanuman, the monkey-king who helped Prince Rama rescue his wife.

When the island was called the Isle of Serendib, the voyage of Sinbad was described in the Thousand and One Nights. Medieval Arabs and Persians made regular pilgrimages to Adam's Peak. The fourteenth century Arab traveler and scholar Ibn Batutah made that pilgrimage.

Legends record the visit of the Qutb ☉ who after visiting Adam's Peak meditated for twelve years in what came to be known as the hermitage shrine of Daftar Jailani that lies at the edge of a precipitous granite cliff in the south central portion of the island, a site that has become a place of saintly visitation and mystical meditation.

Living in that land of legends, those seekers from Kokuvil recognized Bawa Muhaiyaddeen ☉ as a uniquely mystical being when they began to interact with him, begging him to teach them. He had lived peacefully alone in the jungle for so long that he had almost forgotten human speech. Gradually, he began to speak with those seekers.

Telling those seekers that God was the only Teacher, he consented only to study side by side with them. Working long hours in the rice fields as a farmer by day and giving away the rice to poor people, he spoke and sang to them of his experiences of God in the evenings. Eventually, he and that small group of seekers from Kokuvil built an ashram in Jaffna, a town in the northern tip of the country.

Travel was difficult in that small country, yet the refuge of his presence was irresistible. As more and more people came to know about him and to hear him sing and speak of God, many of them began to invite him to stay in their homes. Among those people were Dr. Ajwad Macan-Markar and his wife Ameen Macan-Markar who lived in the city of Colombo. Bawa Muhaiyaddeen ☉ told them it would not be easy: that he was like a tree upon which many birds needed to take shelter. If he was to agree to stay at their home, they would also have to accommodate these birds. He warned them that there could be many at times. Dr. Ajwad and his wife did not hesitate to agree to open their home to all who wished to accompany him. After that, Bawa Muhaiyaddeen ☉ always stayed at their home when he was in Colombo. For forty years Bawa Muhaiyaddeen ☉ spent his time with those seekers until 1971.

In *The Tree That Fell to the West*,[1] Bawa Muhaiyaddeen ☉ tells us:

"Before I arrived at 46th Street in Philadelphia for my first visit, Bob Demby, Carolyn Secretary [Carolyn Andrews], Zoharah Simmons and some others sitting here arranged for me to come.

"They formed a society for that purpose, to invite me here. I did not come to Philadelphia with the idea of establishing a fellowship. There is only one Fellowship and that is Allāh's. There is only one family and one Fellowship. We are all the children of Adam ☉, and Allāh is in charge of that Fellowship."

After that first visit, Bawa Muhaiyaddeen ☉ went back and forth between Philadelphia and what by then had been renamed Sri Lanka until 1982, when he stayed in the United States until December 1986.

---
1 Muhaiyaddeen, Bawa. *The Tree That Fell to the West*. Philadelphia: Fellowship Press, 2003. Print.

In these distressing times, his words are increasingly recognized as representing the original intention of Islām which is the purity of the relationship between man and God as explained by all the prophets of God, from Adam, Noah, Abraham, Ishmael, Moses, David, Jesus, and Muhammad, may the peace of God be upon them, who were all sent to tell and retell mankind that there is one and only One God, and that this One is their Source—attainable, and waiting for the return of each individual soul.

Publications

Books

Islam, Jerusalem, and World Peace: Explanations of a Sufi
website: islamjerusalemandworld peace.org

Prayer

Al-Asmā'ul Husnā: The Duties and Qualities of Allāh
website: asmaulhusna.org

The Choice

Bawa Asks Bawa Muhaiyaddeen ☺ (Volumes One, Two & Three)

Life Is a Dream: A Book of Sufi Verse

A Timeless Treasury of Sufi Quotations

The Four Virtues and Their Relationship to Good Behavior and Bad Conduct

Sūratur-Rahmah: The form of Compassion

God's Psychology: A Sufi Explanation

The Point Where God and Man Meet

The Map of the Journey to God: Lessons from the School of Grace

The Golden Words of a Sufi Sheikh, Revised Edition

A Book of God's Love

The Resonance of Allah: Resplendent Explanations Arising from the *Nūr, Allāh's* Wisdom of Grace

The Tree That Fell to the West: Autobiography of a Sufi

Questions of Life — Answers of Wisdom (Volumes One & Two)

The Fast of Ramadan: The Inner Heart Blossoms

Hajj: The Inner Pilgrimage

The Triple Flame: The Inner Secrets of Sufism

A Song of Muhammad ☺

To Die Before Death: The Sufi Way of Life

A Mystical Journey

Sheikh and Disciple

Why Can't I See the Angels: Children's Questions to a Sufi Saint

Treasures of the Heart: Sufi Stories for Young Children

Come to the Secret Garden: Sufi Tales of Wisdom

My Love You My Children: 101 Stories for Children of All Ages
Maya Veeram or The Forces of Illusion
God, His Prophets and His Children
Four Steps to Pure *Īmān*
The Wisdom of Man
Truth & Light: Brief Explanations
Songs of God's Grace
The Guidebook to the True Secret of the Heart (Volumes One & Two)
The Divine Luminous Wisdom That Dispels the Darkness
Wisdom of the Divine (Volumes One to Six)
The Tasty, Economical Cookbook, Second Edition

Booklets

Beyond Creation
Can We Ever Regain Our Innocence?
Come to Prayer: The Wake-up Song
Duʿāʾ Kanzul-'arsh (The Invocation of the Treasure of the Throne)
An Explanation of the Benefits of Reciting the *Salawāt*
The Foot of the Qutb ☉
The Hospital Story
King Solomon ☉ and the Fish & Explanations about Jinns and Fairies
The Opening of the Mosque of Shaikh M. R. Bawa Muhaiyaddeen ☉
Sindanay & I Will Tell You of the Way
Sufism
Why We Recite the Maulids

A Contemporary Sufi Speaks Series

On the Meaning of Fellowship
Mind, Desire, and the Billboards of the World
On Peace of Mind
On the Signs of Destruction
Teenagers and Parents
On the True Meaning of Sufism
On Unity: The Legacy of the Prophets

Gems of Wisdom series:
Vol. 1: The Value of Good Qualities
Vol. 2: Beyond Mind and Desire
Vol. 3: The Innermost Heart
Vol. 4: Come to Prayer

The Instructions
The Fox and the Crocodile and Do Not Carry Tales
God Is Very Light
Prayer: Starting Over
Unity

Pamphlets
Advice to Prisoners
Faith
The Golden Words of a Sufi Sheikh: Preface to the Book
Grieving for the Dead
Keep the Pond Clean
Letter to the World Family
Love Is the Remedy, God Is the Healer
Marriage
A Prayer for Father's Day
A Prayer for My Children
A Prayer from My Heart
Strive for a Good Life
Sufi: A Brief Explanation
A Sufi Perspective on Business
25 Duties – The True Meaning of Fellowship
Who Is God?
With Every Breath, Say *Lā Ilāha Ill-Allāhu*
Why Man Has No Peace (from My Love You, My Children)
The Wisdom and Grace of the Sufis

Foreign Language Publications

Ein Zeitgenössischer Sufi Spricht über Inneren Frieden
Deux Discours tirés du Livre L'Islam et la Paix Mondiale:
Explications d'un Soufi
La Paix
Quién Es Dios? Una Explicatión por el Sheikh Sufi

Other Publications

Bawa Muhaiyaddeen Fellowship Calendar
Morning *Dhikr* at the Mosque of Shaikh M. R. Bawa Muhaiyaddeen ☺
Songs of Divine Wisdom
(a notated version of songs by M. R. Bawa Muhaiyaddeen ☺)
The *Subhāna Maulid*

Stream the Teachings

http://s3.nexuscast.com/start/bmfdd/
The Daily Discourse: the teachings of Bawa Muhaiyaddeen ☺ in chronological order, every even hour on the hour, Eastern Time [GMT-5].

http://sc1.mystreamserver.com/start/bmfhs/
Live from the Fellowship House and Mosque: morning *dhikr*, five-times prayer, Bawa Muhaiyaddeen's discourses and songs, meetings, and special events.

http://s3.nexuscast.com/start/bmf786/
24/7 Radio: a continuous stream of over 300 discourses and songs from the CD of the Month, updated every Anniversary Weekend.

WE INVITE YOU TO VISIT

The Fellowship in Philadelphia, Pennsylvania, the place where Bawa Muhaiyaddeen ☻ stayed when he visited the United States, continues to serve as a meeting house and a reservoir of materials for everyone wishing access to his teachings.

The Mosque of Shaikh M. R. Bawa Muhaiyaddeen ☻ is located on the same property as the Fellowship. The five daily prayers and Friday congregational prayers are observed.

The Mazār, the resting place of Bawa Muhaiyaddeen ☻, is an hour west of the Fellowship and open daily between sunrise and sunset.

email: info@bmf.org
website: www.bmf.org/publications

For further information about visiting, Fellowship events, branch locations, and meetings:
The Bawa Muhaiyaddeen Fellowship
5820 Overbrook Avenue
Philadelphia, Pennsylvania 19131
Phone: (215) 879-6300
Fax: (215) 879-6307

For book information: **(888) 786-1786**
To order CDs and DVDs: **www.bmfstore.com**

Al-hamdu lillāh, all praise is due to God!